M000038944

Creating Character

Bringing Your Story to Life

Creating Character: Bringing Your Story to Life

First Edition

Copyright © 2013 William Bernhardt Writing Programs

Published by the Red Sneaker Press

An imprint of Babylon Books

All rights reserved

ISBN: 978-0-9893789-0-1

No part of this book may be reproduced, scanned, or

distributed in any printed or electronic form without

permission. Please do not participate in or encourage piracy

of copyrighted materials in violation of the author's rights.

Purchase only authorized editions.

Creating Character
Bringing Your Story to Life

William Bernhardt

The Red Sneaker Writer Series

Other Books by William Bernhardt

Red Sneaker Writer Series

Story Structure: The Key to Successful Fiction
Creating Character: Bringing Your Story to Life
Perfect Plotting: Charting the Hero's Journey
Dynamic Dialogue: Letting Your Story Speak
The Fundamentals of Fiction (DVD)

The Ben Kincaid Series

Primary Justice
Blind Justice
Deadly Justice
Perfect Justice
Cruel Justice
Naked Justice
Extreme Justice
Dark Justice
Silent Justice

Murder One
Criminal Intent
Hate Crime
Death Row
Capitol Murder
Capitol Threat
Capitol Conspiracy
Capitol Offense
Capitol Betrayal

Other Novels

The Code of Buddhood
Paladins of the Abyss
Dark Eye
The Midnight Before Christmas
Final Round
Double Jeopardy

Nemesis: The Final Case of Eliot Ness
Strip Search
The Idea Man
Shine

For Young Readers

Equal Justice: The Courage of Ada Lois Sipuel (biography)
Princess Alice and the Dreadful Dragon (illustrated by Kerry McGhee)
The Black Sentry

Edited by William Bernhardt

Legal Briefs
Natural Suspect

Dedicated to all the Red Sneaker Writers:
You can't fail unless you quit.

Action is character.

Aristotle

TABLE OF CONTENTS

INTRODUCTION

Welcome to the world of the Red Sneaker Writers. If you're familiar with this outfit or you've read other Red Sneaker publications or attended Red Sneaker events, you can skip to Chapter One. If you're new, let me take a moment to explain.

I've been writing a long time, and I've been speaking at writing workshops and conferences almost as long. Every time I take to the stage I see the same tableau staring back at me: long rows of talented people, most of whom have attended many conferences, frustrated by the fact that they can't sell a book. And wondering why. Yes, the market is tough and agents are hard to find yadda yadda yadda whine whine whine excuse excuse excuse. But when aspiring writers do the work, put it out there, but still don't publish…there's usually a reason. Too often enormous potential is lost due to a lack of fundamental knowledge. Sometimes a little vigorous instruction is all that stands between an unpublished writer and a satisfying writing career.

I always do my best to help at conferences, but the large auditorium/general information lecture is not terribly conducive to writing instruction. And sometimes what I've heard other instructors say was not particularly helpful. Too often people seemed more interested in obfuscating writing and appearing "literary" than in providing useful information. Sometimes I felt speakers were determined to make writing as mysterious and incomprehensible as possible, either because that made them sound more erudite or because they didn't understand the subject themselves. How is that going to help anyone get published?

After giving this problem some thought, I formulated the Red Sneaker Writing Center. Why Red Sneakers? Because I love my red sneakers. They're practical, flexible, sturdy—and bursting with style and flair. In other words, exactly what I think writing instruction should be. Practical, flexible, useful, but still designed to unleash the creative spirit, to give the imagination a platform for creating wondrous work.

I started reaching out to other Red Sneaker Writers with an annual conference. I invited the best teachers I knew, not only people who had published many books but people who knew how to share their knowledge. Then I launched my small group seminars—five intensive days of work with a handful of aspiring writers. This gave me the opportunity to read, edit, and work one-on-one with individuals so I could target their needs and make sure they got what would help them most. This approach worked extremely well and I'm proud to say a substantial list of writers have graduated from my seminars and published work with major publishers. But not everyone is able to fly to my seminars, and I couldn't justify traveling all over the world to work with one or two writers. What to do?

This book, and the other books in the Red Sneaker Writer series, are designed to address that problem. Short inexpensive books providing the help people need. Let me see if I can anticipate your questions:

Why are they so short? I've tried to expunge the unnecessary. I'm paring it down to the essential information, practical and useful ideas that can improve your writing. Too many educational books are padded to fill word counts. That's not the Red Sneaker way.

Why so many different books instead of one big book? I encourage writers to write every day and maintain a schedule (see Appendix B). You can read these books without losing a lot of writing time. In fact, each can be read in a single afternoon. Take one day off from your writing schedule. Read and make notes in the margins. See if this doesn't trigger ideas for your own work.

I bet it will. And the next day, you can get back to your writing schedule.

Why does each chapter end with exercises? Is this just padding?

No. The exercises are a completely integrated and essential part of this book. Samuel Johnson was correct when he wrote: *Scribendo disces scribere*. Meaning: You learn to write by writing. I can gab on and on in my incredibly intelligent way, but it won't be concretized in your brain until you put it into practice. So don't get in such a hurry that you don't get the full benefit out of this book. Take the time to complete the assignments, because it may improve your next writing effort.

I also send out a free monthly newsletter filled with writing advice, market analysis, and other items of interest to Red Sneaker Writers. If you'd like to be added to the mailing list, you can sign up for it at my website: www.williambernhardt.com. You may also be interested in my DVD set, *The Fundamentals of Fiction*, available at Amazon or on my website. It's about five hours of me talking about writing. Who doesn't want that?

Okay, enough of this warm-up act. Read this book. Then write something wonderful.

William Bernhardt

CHAPTER 1: CHARACTER IS CRITICAL

What is character but the illumination of incident, and what is incident but the illumination of character?
Henry James

Memorable characters are the most essential hallmark of enduring fiction. Not to say there aren't other elements of import. Structure is important. Narrative movement is important. Most people prefer a story with a plot that engages their imagination. Many readers enjoy a book with a vivid setting, one that transports them to worlds they've never seen before. Every reader has experienced that glorious epiphany or vicarious thrill that comes from realizing the book in their hands illuminates one of life's great mysteries. Who hasn't laughed or cried over a book that provided a spectacular emotional experience, that made you feel better about humankind?

But it all starts with character.

If people aren't interested in your main character, nothing else matters. You can put the protagonist through all kinds of emotional trials. We will not feel for him. You can run your character through breathtaking cliffhangers, amazing derring-do, and the narrowest of escapes. No one's heart will beat any faster. You can address the great themes, but it will come off as a lecture. For a story to work, the reader must relate at some level with your primary character. Which does not mean the character must be perfect, admirable, or even terribly likeable (though that can help).

Your character must be interesting. Your character must be memorable.

Which is very easy to say and much harder to do. So let's discuss how you can do it and bring your fiction to life.

The Myth of Character vs. Plot

Too often, I hear people talk about character and plot as if they were completely different entities. They are not. They are simply two different ways of looking at the same thing: your story. As the quote from Henry James suggests, character and plot are two sides of the same coin, two ways of illuminating the same subject matter. This being the case, considering one apart from the other makes no sense. Too often snobby creative writing classes teach that some fiction is character-driven and some fiction is plot-driven. Wrong.

All fiction is character-driven. All of it. Even books you may think have paper-thin characterization but rip-snorting plots. They are all character-driven.

I have written many books featuring the character Ben Kincaid, a likeable nebbish of a lawyer, driven but emotionally repressed, caring but perpetually awkward around other people (especially women). The first book in the series, *Primary Justice*, was a straightforward mystery novel. In later outings, I added more courtroom drama and later still more thriller elements. But every book involved some mysterious death, and every book involved Ben Kincaid figuring out who did it. So perhaps you will not be surprised that critics often refer to crime fiction as "plot-driven."

Now ask yourself this question: Why would anyone pick up the eighteenth book in a "plot-driven" crime series? Are they so desperate to read about another murder? Is there any question about whether the mystery will be solved? Is it the orgasmic thrill they get when they hear Ben's stirring closing argument?

I don't think so, though that might boost my sales figures. No, the only reason people would pick up the eighteenth book in any series is because they care about the *character*. They like spending time with him and they want to see what happens to him next.

Series fiction has become increasingly popular in recent years. Here I don't mean a real series, that is, a continued story that spills over several books, like Tolkien's *The Lord of the Rings* or Martin's A *Song of Fire and Ice*. I mean books that are actually self-contained but use a continuing character or characters. Lee Child's Jack Reacher. Steve Berry's Cotton Malone. Laurel Hamilton's Anita Blake. Jim Butcher's Harry Dresden. And so forth. There was a time when series characters were treated dismissively or associated with dime novels of the lowest literary ilk. That day has long passed. Today publishers in some genres are reluctant to sign an author unless there is a prior commitment to additional books featuring the same character.

Why do publishers, authors, and readers like series characters so much? Because they're plot insurance. By using a series character, the author in effect takes out an insurance policy to protect against the possibility that you might not be all that intrigued by the storyline for this particular outing. Were this a standalone novel, even one coming from an author you've enjoyed in the past, you might read the plot description on the back cover, find it faintly familiar, and think, Nah. I'll wait for the next one.

But if it features a character you like, your reaction might be, Well, I have to see what's going on with Ben. Don't want to miss anything important. Maybe he'll finally tie the knot with Christina or make amends with his mother…and so forth.

So with a series character, the publishers get the best of both worlds. Each book remains self-contained, so they avoid the problem of readers feeling they must read the books in publication order. But they maintain the feeling that fans must pick up each new story featuring this character.

All of this, of course, only works if people enjoy reading about your character. If they find the character flat, clichéd, uninteresting, commonplace, or unexciting, you not only will not get a series, you probably won't get published.

Don't worry. We're going to discuss how to create memorable characters, or to tweak the ones you have to make them more memorable.

The Myth of Literary or "Character-Driven" Fiction

At one time or another, you may have heard someone suggest that so-called literary fiction is character-driven while popular or genre fiction is plot-driven—probably someone with a graduate degree in English. (I can say that, because I have one, too.) Given what you just read, you've probably already surmised that I disagree. I not only disagree, I think this is arrant nonsense that obfuscates rather than illuminates the true distinctions between different kinds of books. And I say that speaking as someone who has read voraciously my entire life. I've read and enjoyed most of the Great Books and survived to tell the tale. And there are differences between, say, *The Taming of the Shrew* and *The Hunger Games*. But the differences aren't about character, because they both have great characters. And the differences aren't about plot either, because both tell fascinating stories. So what's the diff?

Literary fiction is sometimes called "plotless" because the character's quest is largely or entirely internal, that is, the character is seeking love, or truth, or spirituality, rather than the Holy Grail or the identity of the murderer. The best literary fiction often has a discernable and engaging plot. And a strong plot will catapult literary fiction to the top of the charts.

Let's consider some critically acclaimed and popular literary novels. The Man Booker Prize was awarded to *Room* by Emma Donoghue. The plot involves an abducted woman who is locked in a room and sexually abused. She eventually gives birth and raises the child in the titular room...until Plot Point 1 (see discussion of plot points in the book on Structure). This could easily be the plot of a crime novel, and in fact, has been on several prior occasions. In Cormac McCarthy's *The Road*, a Pulitzer Prize and Oprah Book Club winner, a father and son travel in search of a safe haven in a hideous post-apocalyptic America. This could easily be the plot of a science fiction novel, and in fact, has been on several prior occasions. Karen Thompson Walker's novel *The Age of Miracles* also tells an end-of-the-world story. How can we say books with such high-concept, dynamic plotlines are character-driven fiction?

What distinguishes these and other literary novels is not the presence of better characters nor the absence of plot. The hallmarks are a more poetic approach to language and the absence of narrative urgency. In literary fiction, the author typically employs less immediate, more artful language. Popular fiction is primarily dominated by the descendants of Hemingway. Whether you like his work or you don't, you must admit that Hemingway has tremendously influenced the style of the writers who followed him. This style is characterized by brevity, directness, and simplicity—which means stripping away the unnecessary but does not mean "dumbing-down." Literary writers may take a more leisurely or stylized approach, often employing memorable turns of phrases or insightful uses of language. But not always. The aforementioned Cormac McCarthy's style is at times so stark he makes Hemingway look like a blabbermouth. But there is still a profound attention to language, with every word being carefully chosen.

The other hallmark of literary fiction is a lack of narrative urgency. The best popular novels hook you from the first page and never let you go until the story is over. That's because the conflict seems dramatic, with high stakes and a ticking clock. That's urgency. That's what forces the reader to keep turning the pages. That's what causes people to stay up all night finishing the book. Does this require less skill than writing literary fiction? Not in my opinion (and if you think so, try writing a page-turner yourself). When you hear someone say, "I couldn't put it down," that doesn't mean the author is a hack who only cares about plot. That means the writer took great care in perfecting and streamlining their language to convey the essential information about both character and plot without slowing the pace of the story. This takes enormous skill and careful revision.

CREATING CHARACTER

But here's the bottom line: **Regardless of what kind of story you are writing, memorable characters are essential.**

We have not always divided books up into literary and popular categories. This false dichotomy arose around the end of the nineteenth century, as English emerged as a department in universities, teaching not the language but the literature. Since reading novels was enormously popular outside the university, a different approach was needed to justify academic attention. Thus began the idea that some books are inherently better than others. The enormous literary experimentation that distinguished the modernist and postmodernist periods fueled this split. (Some would argue that writers deliberately made their work obscure to make it more popular with academia, something James Joyce frequently admitted.)

I believe we will see some of these old tropes disappear. Divisions make us weaker, not stronger, and this distinction benefits no one. How can writers as fine as Dennis Lehane or Elmore Leonard be dismissed as mere "crime writers?" (I won't list them, but there are many so-called literary writers who don't write half so well.) Michael Chabon, the Pulitzer Prize-winning novelist, has proposed a new genre he calls "trickster fiction," which maintains high standards of language while embracing entertainment plots and characters associated with genre fiction. This seems to me the pathway to a more purposeful and dynamic approach to literature for the twenty-first century.

Whether you accept these arguments or not, I hope you will accept the need for strong, dynamic, unique characters in your stories. So start creating them now. The next three chapters will discuss some preliminary matters that might improve your understanding of character and characterization. The remaining chapters will guide you in plumbing the depths of your creativity to unearth characters that will bring your stories to life.

CREATING CHARACTER

Highlights

1) Regardless of what kind of story you are writing, memorable characters are essential.

2) All stories are character-driven.

3) Character and plot are two closely interrelated ways of viewing the same thing: your story.

Red Sneaker Exercises

1) If you have not yet started writing your book, or even if you have, make a writing schedule. Commit to writing a certain number of hours per day (as many as possible) and a certain number of days a week (preferably seven). Now treat that commitment as you would any other job. Show up on time and do what you promised to do. At the end of this book, in Appendix B, you will find a suggested Writing Schedule. See if you can make it your own. Then check out the Writers Contract attached as Appendix C. If you sign it (and if you're serious about writing, you should), it will be legally binding, because it was drafted by an actual attorney. Me.

2) Think about the protagonist in your book. What makes that character interesting, intriguing, or unique? Too often, aspiring novelists make the mistake of basing the main character on themselves. While this might be easier than creating someone from scratch, it is not necessarily the way to come up with a character another person would want to read about. Consider which of your traits are

13

actually essential or useful to this character. One or two, probably. Keep those, but open your mind to the possibility of filling the character out with other traits that will increase reader interest.

CHAPTER 2: CHARACTER AS METAPHOR

In the faces of men and women, I see God.
Walt Whitman

Some of the worst writing advice I've ever heard is this canard: Make it real. Why? Do we not have enough reality in our own lives? Do we really think that's why people pick up a novel—because they want more reality? If readers want more real, they can pick up the newspaper, or worse, turn on the evening news. People read stories because they want something better.

Sometimes I hear writers suggest that because their novel supposedly hews more closely to actual police procedure or courtroom rules, that automatically makes it better. Not necessarily true. Or the writer says that because his book is grittier, or the characters are darker, or everyone behaves in a generally ugly way, the book is more realistic (and therefore better). Makes you wonder what their world looks like—and makes you never want to go there. For instance, I've heard writers of hardboiled PI mysteries talk at length about how their books are more "realistic" than cozy mysteries. Here's a heads up: Neither is remotely realistic, nor does any reader want it to be.

People turn to fiction because they're looking for something better than real life. Granted, the story must have *verisimilitude*—a word first applied to literature by Edgar Allan Poe. This does not mean it must be realistic.

Think about some of Poe's best-known stories. They're not remotely realistic, but he makes the world in which the story arises familiar enough that you will suspend your disbelief and be gripped by the tale. Verisimilitude means "life-like," not real. In other words, the world of the story must be internally consistent. It must make sense within the context of that tale. There must be a credible foundation from which the fantasy springs forth. But realistic? No.

In fiction, readers look for something better and more satisfying than what real life typically yields, even if they are not aware that this is what motivates them. Novels provide an orderly structured narrative. Real life rarely does. Novels have a discernible beginning, middle, and end. When the novel ends, it usually provides a sense of closure, so often missing from real-life experience. In America, a novel typically ends in a positive, upbeat fashion, and more importantly, leaves you with an emotional uplift or reward. This does happen in life on occasion, but not nearly as often as we'd like. And that's why we read novels.

So if your mother advised you to "write what you know," ignore her. (Though you should remember her advice about "playing nice with others.") Your touchstone should not be "write what you know," but rather, "write what interests you." Write what you would want to read. If we literally only wrote about what was real, what we know, we'd have no *Beowulf*, no *Odyssey*, no Poe, no Verne, no Wells, no *1984*, no *Brave New World*, no Bradbury. And the world would be a much poorer place. Instead, illuminate what we know—by writing a story that captures a reader's imagination.

And the first step in capturing a reader's attention is creating a character with whom the reader would like to spend time.

CREATING CHARACTER

Your Characters Are Not Real

Few things make me despair so much as when I hear some sweet well-meaning pre-published writer tell me that he started writing his book and then "the characters took over." This may sound wonderfully romantic, particularly if you spend a lot of time listening to authors on television talking about writing (which is almost uniformly unreliable). But the first problem is that this suggests you have done little prior thinking about your characters or your plot, and if you've read my book on Structure you know just how lethal that can be. The second problem is that it suggests the writer is entertaining himself but lacks the discipline to actually finish something others might want to read. And the third problem, my friends, is that your characters are not real. They only exist in your head (until someone else reads your book). You can't "take over" yourself. You've been in control all along.

Just as novels are not reality, your characters are not real people, and contrary to what you may think, you don't want them to be. You may want them to be realistic, to have verisimilitude, but you do not want them to be real. You want your characters to be something better, something larger. You want your characters to represent something greater than any one person, even yourself.

Characters are not real people. They are metaphors.

A metaphor, as you'll recall from freshman English, is something that represents something else, typically something greater or more intangible. The cross represents spirituality. The valentine-shaped heart represents love. The blanket represents comfort. The road sign represents destiny.

Like your characters, the Statue of Liberty is not a real woman. She's a metaphor, a fairly obvious one. What does she represent? Liberty, of course. Freedom. Second chances. New beginnings. A fresh start. Welcoming arms. "Give me your tired, your poor/Your huddled masses yearning to breathe free/The wretched refuse of your teeming shores…"

Personally, I wouldn't care to be called anyone's "wretched refuse." But were I a poor half-starving German-born Russian immigrant, as my great-grandfather was, I might not mind so much. I would gaze at that beautiful green lady and see a glorious opportunity to improve my family's prospects. I would be inspired by this opportunity to improve my life.

Because that's what metaphors do.

Your characters, particularly your main character (the protagonist), can also be metaphors. In fact, they should be. In the best books, they *will* be.

Let's consider some of the most popular, most enduring characters in the history of literature. Whenever I ask people to name their favorite character, the name that comes up most frequently is Scarlett O'Hara (from *Gone With the Wind*, of course). Why is Scarlett so popular? I think it's fair to say she's not perfect. In some respects, she's not even very nice. As the book opens, she is completely selfish, self-absorbed, and cares only about the least important aspects of life. She's a flirt, a tease, and a bit of a shrew. When the war hits, she matures considerably, but she hardly becomes a saint. She's greedy, manipulative, and sometimes cruel. She marries men for money, which some would say is about as low as a person can sink. Why do people like this horrible woman so much?

She's not boring. First and foremost. She's unique, interesting, and always fun to watch. She's not all bad, either. As the book progresses, she shows courage, fortitude, grit, and determination. She may not be perfect, but she keeps that plantation together. And she never gives up. Tomorrow is another day.

Scarlett O'Hara is a metaphor. To her readers, she represents strength and courage under fire (when it is most needed). She embodies virtues readers admire and hope they will display when life decides to test them, as it almost certainly will. She's a survivor.

Sherlock Holmes is one of the most popular fictional characters in history, known all around the world. He has been portrayed in more movies than any other single character. And yet, like Scarlett, he is not altogether a likeable person. He can be rude, even abrasive. Condescending. Arrogant. Treats poor Lestrade like an idiot. Horrible with women. This man's mother, if indeed he had one, did not give him the lesson about playing nice with others. So why do readers find him so fascinating?

Because he's smart. No matter what else happens, his brain is bigger than anyone else's. Only Moriarty comes close, but even he cannot defeat the brilliant Holmes. In other words, Holmes is a metaphor for the power of intelligence, for the triumph of brain over brawn. In real life, it may seem as if the world is run by bullies and brutes and bureaucratic tools. But in the world of Holmes, the smarter man always wins the day.

Like Scarlett O'Hara, Holmes is a metaphor for something readers find appealing, either because it represents the world as they see it, or because it represents the world as they would like it to be.

Who are your favorite characters? Why? Chances are they represent some appealing quality or virtue that endeared them to you—even if you weren't conscious of it when you read the book.

Who are the other best-known characters of the last hundred years or so? James Bond—the emotionally cool superspy supercharged with both machismo and savoir-faire. Harry Potter—the innocent youth determined to sacrifice himself for others. Superman—the savior from another planet who has powers sufficient to rule the world, but instead chooses to serve. Tarzan—the embodiment of triumph over a difficult childhood. Though orphaned and alone in darkest Africa, this British lord ends up running the joint.

All these characters serve as metaphors for qualities people find appealing. Strength. Courage. Intelligence. Service to others. Determination. Style.

What does your main character represent? Something wonderful, I hope.

You Are Not Your Character

I alluded earlier to the fact that most people setting out to write their first book will base the lead character upon themselves. This may be the product of a poor imagination. It may simply be a matter of convenience—writing about the person you know best. It may be a matter of ego—who would you rather think about? But you shouldn't be thinking about yourself at all, at least not at first. You should be thinking: What character would be best for the story I want to tell? What character would best embody the virtues or ideals I want my story to represent?

CREATING CHARACTER

What metaphor do I want to instill in my reader's subconscious?

Once you know the answers to those questions, inventing your protagonist should be duck soup. Once you know what their greatest strengths or assets are, the rest is filling in the details—in the most interesting manner possible. Some of this will be dictated by the time and place of your story. (And just as you don't automatically base your character on yourself, you shouldn't automatically set your story in the town where you live, another sign that you may be writing your ego rather than writing your story).

Your main characters should have lives and you should know those lives from start to finish, which is why I suggest that you complete a Character Detail Sheet or resume or Facebook page for your main characters (see Appendix A). You should know your primary characters' lives from cradle to grave. And once you have that thorough understanding of your characters' lives, their backstory, where they are now, and where they are headed, it will be much easier to extract the moments from their lives that will advance the story you want to tell.

Basically, the information you want to know inside and out about your main characters can be divided into five categories: **Background, Personality, Appearance, Occupation,** and **Secret Identity**.

Let's start with **Background**, since that will inform so many of the other categories. Where did this character come from? City or rural? One parent, two parents, or none? Got along with them or didn't? Happy childhood or sad? Lots of friends or none? While all people are different, we can't deny that parents have a huge role in shaping their children's characters, consciously or unconsciously, in a positive or a negative way. Siblings, friends, and relatives

21

can be equally important. A character who grew up in a large loving family with a stay-at-home mother in a small town is likely to be markedly different from a child of a single working mother attending a large urban school with cliques and bullies. I don't think you can really know who your character is unless you know where they came from.

Which leads to **Personality**, which could also be called Behavior. Remember, personality is not necessarily a function of who your character really is, but rather, how that character chooses to behave. How they present themselves in public. Sometimes the shyest people on Earth have learned to put on an outgoing public persona. But personality can lend insight into inner character, and books usually benefit from having characters whose personalities complement without duplicating one another. If your protagonist is idealistic and serious, you may want a sidekick who is practical and wisecracking. People with differing personalities will react to conflict in different ways, thus enriching your story.

Appearance may seem the least important and most superficial of these categories, but as I will discuss later in the chapter on Characterization, how your character looks may tell us a good deal about who that character really is. Clothes and grooming can yield enormous insights. We all know that the same guy can dress himself as an emo loner or a rugged jock. The same girl can dress herself as a chic preppie or a tramp. The character's choice each morning when they open the clothes closet should provide insight into their personality, as should their hairstyle, their accessories, their makeup or lack thereof, their posture, etc. Try to think of your character in three dimensions. How do they choose to fill the space they occupy in your fictional universe?

Occupation concerns more than just what they do for a living, though that is an important component. Also remember to consider what they do in their spare time. Do they have hobbies? Do they play sports? Do they hang with friends? Or are they introspective? Do they quietly reflect upon their life? Do they meditate? Do they like to solve the morning puzzle? Listen to music as they drive to work? All these factors involve choices, and those choices should give the reader insight into the character.

Then there is the **Secret Identity**. You may think your character doesn't have one, and if so, I'm going to suggest that you haven't thought deeply enough about the character. We all have secret identities. Not necessarily of the Clark Kent variety, but something that is not immediately apparent to others, something that perhaps even our best friends and those closest to us do not know. Everyone has secrets. More than anything else, this secret identity may get to the central question of character creation: *Who are you?*

Before I wrote *Primary Justice*, the first of the Ben Kincaid books, I had a CHARACTER DETAIL SHEET I'd obtained at a conference somewhere. I took the time to fill it out for Ben and Christina and some of the other major characters. By the time I was done, I knew Ben's life from start to finish. Most of that never appeared in a book. But it did help me obtain a clear view of who this person was so I could do a more consistent job of writing him. Little did I know that *Primary Justice* would be a huge hit and that I would write many more books starring that character. All that work I invested in understanding Ben's life paid off.

At this point, you may be asking yourself, what does Ben Kincaid represent? Is he a metaphor? Let me take you

23

back to the time of his creation, back in the 1980s, well before Grisham and others made lawyers hot literary properties. At that time, the best-known fictional lawyer (perhaps the only well-known fictional lawyer) was Perry Mason. What did Perry Mason represent? As far as I was concerned, the answer was: Perfection. Perry Mason never lost a case. (Technically, he lost one, but later got it reversed.) Perry had all the answers. Perry displayed no strong emotions. He had no personal relationships. He was so good in the courtroom, he not only won, he got villains to confess on the witness stand. Would you like to know how often that happens in real life? Never. So much for realism. And yet, this character's godlike perfection was clearly part of his appeal. For readers and viewers, Perry Mason represented justice. Truth. The soundness of the American legal system.

I have a different view of the American legal system. So I created a different metaphor.

Ben Kincaid is basically everything Perry Mason is not. He's not perfect. He's not flawless. He doesn't have all the answers. He's not emotionless. He's not psychologically unscarred. At first, he's not even very good in the courtroom. Get witnesses to confess? He can barely speak aloud without stuttering. So why would anyone read about this loser?

I think it's because there are some people out there who feel more like Ben than Perry.

Ben may not be perfect, but he always tries to do the right thing. He genuinely cares about his clients. He goes the extra mile. Even when the odds are stacked against him (and they usually are), he never quits. Let me say that again. *He never quits.* And even though he's shy, emotionally reserved, perhaps even a bit neurotic, and completely useless around women—he's very smart.

That's a character some readers could admire. Someone they could even root for.

Ben represents the underdog. The guy who isn't perfect, isn't a big smoothie, isn't always right—but his heart is always in the right place. Ben represents the rebel, the guy who isn't content to go along with a malfunctioning system, but instead finds ways to make it better. He's constantly compensating for the enormous flaws and injustices perpetrated by the American legal system.

To my admittedly prejudiced mind, Ben is a much more American hero than Perry Mason. Because Americans have always been underdogs and rebels. Americans are always looking for a way to make the world better than it is.

That's the metaphor I think Ben Kincaid embodies, though it's entirely possible that some readers see it differently. It's more likely that most readers liked the character without giving conscious thought to exactly why. But spoken or unspoken, the emotional appeal of the metaphor is what endears readers to a character. It's what gives a character resonance even larger than what is printed on the page.

It can do the same for you. So take the time to get to know your character, inside and out. But never lose sight of what your character *represents*.

Basing Your Characters on Real People

While we're in the neighborhood, let's discuss the problem of basing characters on people you know. I probably don't need to tell you that since most beginning writers tend to base their protagonist on themselves, they tend to populate the supporting cast with other known entities, like their parents, their children, their boss, their mother-in-law, etc. This is not a good idea.

Until you've actually had a book in print, you cannot imagine what a galvanizing effect it will have on your world, how the people you know personally see you, and how they read your work. I didn't help anything by setting my first book in a law firm at a time when I worked in a law firm, but I'd heard that bad advice about writing what you know, and I couldn't think of anything else that I knew anything about. So I set my book in a law firm, careful at all times to distinguish my characters from the real people I knew.

And it made no difference whatsoever. Even before the book was released, I started hearing the myriad rampant theories about who the characters "*really* were." I probably heard ten different interpretations of who every major character was based upon, all of them conflicting, and each proponent absolutely adamant they had properly decoded the book. This is perhaps understandable. People like to think they've got the inside track, that they have secret knowledge others do not. I had people I barely knew running around explaining who my characters were, based upon their non-existent knowledge of my life and me. Frustrating, especially when you'd rather people appreciated the work you put into developing three-dimensional characters. The determination of some people to spread gossip is a force stronger than gravity. You can't stop it.

But you can at least avoid giving them any undue ammunition. So don't base your characters on real people. Which leads to the next question: What do I base them on? Martians?

CREATING CHARACTER

If you know someone who has some salient characteristic that you think would be good for your fictional character, take that characteristic—and only that characteristic. A sassy sense of humor. An arrogant demeanor. Snappy fashion sense. Bipolar disorder. Gold-digging relationships. Self-delusion. Self-doubt. Emotional obliviousness. Take whatever characteristic it is you can use—and nothing else. Then take another characteristic from someone else, and another one from someone else, and add a physical description that looks like none of the sources. And you'll probably be safe.

Here's the sad reality: You cannot prevent people from talking about you or even suing you, particularly sad folk who may see the gossip or the lawsuit as their one chance to snatch a tiny piece of the public eye. And defending a lawsuit, however stupid or baseless, will be expensive. But you can try to avoid the situation by never giving anyone cause to think they've been portrayed in your book.

What if that isn't enough? What if, like Carly Simon's old lover, you think some arrogant SOB will be "so vain you probably think this song is about you?" Here's where you apply what I like to call the "small penis" defense. In other words, you give that character some trait, or better yet several traits, so appallingly undesirable that no one will ever want to sit at the witness stand and say, "Yes, that's me. It's obvious. I am the arrogant smug domineering bastard who also suffers from premature ejaculation, genital warts, and a fondness for angora."

It's possible even that won't be enough. But you'll enjoy the trial a lot more.

Highlights

1) Characters are not real people. They are metaphors.

2) Do not base your protagonist solely upon yourself.

3) Do not base any of your other characters solely upon anyone.

4) Let your main character embody a virtue or principle that connects thematically to what you want your book to represent.

Red Sneaker Exercises

1) Complete the Character Detail Sheet for your protagonist and antagonist using the form attached as Appendix A. Take your time. Do you know as much about these critical characters as you should?

2) You may have heard the term "takeaway," meaning what the reader takes away after reading a book. What will they get from reading *your* book? How will they be rewarded for spending their time with your work? Complete the following sentences:

When readers finish my book, I want them to feel

_____.

CREATING CHARACTER

When readers finish my book, I want them to think
_____.

Given that, what should your protagonist represent? What is your metaphor?

CHAPTER 3: CHARACTER AND CHARACTERIZATION

You cannot dream yourself into a character; you must hammer and forge yourself one.
Henry David Thoreau

Some of the most confused discussions about literary characters I have ever heard resulted from people who could not distinguish character from characterization. Granted, one should inform the other. But they are not the same thing. As a writer, you must understand the difference. Characterization is the tool you use to create these fictional metaphors. Character is the ultimate goal. Or to put it another way:

Characterization is the observable details. Character is who they really are.

Characterization

Characterization may not be as important as character itself, but it is still plenty important. You have probably heard that time-honored truism of writing: show, don't tell. And you may have thought, okay, easy to say, now how exactly do I do that? With regard to character, one answer is characterization, that is, observable details. Sure, you can say the woman was vain and arrogant, but those are just words and are unlikely to have much impact on the reader. On the other hand, if you show the woman driving a sports car she can't afford, or dangling a Michael Kors purse from her elbow, or speaking in an affected accent even though she grew up in rural Arkansas—you've shown who she is without telling. And because you have handled the matter with skill and style, the character will make a much greater impact on your reader.

I could provide any number of examples of this in action, because there are an infinite number of characters out there. Fortunately, the list of potential observable details is equally infinite. Rather than telling your reader who your character is, show them by describing their clothing, their shoes, their car, their luggage. Bring them to life by describing their speech patterns, their mannerisms and affectations. Tell the reader what they order in restaurants or how they treat the doorman. Describe what perfume or cologne they wear. Just make sure that whatever details you provide actually matter.

Characterization should provide insight into who the character really is.

Don't waste the reader's time with details of no importance. Too often, early writers will feel they have to give extended physical descriptions of every character, so they assign physical characteristics more or less at random. After they've described the protagonist in a manner that makes them appear suspiciously like a glamorized version of the author, they describe the other characters with whatever is left. If the last alluring female was blonde, then this one must be brunette (unless she's trouble, in which case she's a redhead). If the last man in the story was tall, then this one must be short, and so forth.

This approach is flawed for two reasons. First, not every character has to be described in extensive physical detail. As I will discuss later, some characters are more important than others. So long as you have a handful of strong, carefully etched characters in the lead, the minor players can come and go without so much attention. Regardless of what you write, most readers will conjure in their mind's eye an image of what a character looks like based upon their own past experiences, what they themselves have encountered or heard or read or seen on television. If you say a character is a coroner, they will immediately think of the last coroner character they encountered. And if the character isn't particularly important, that may be enough. If you stop to provide extensive physical descriptions of each of the seventy or eighty characters passing through a typical novel, the reader will be deluged with an overload of detail and eventually will not be able to envision anything.

Even if you decide that a character is of sufficient import that he or she must be described, that does not mean that every character detail must be dumped upon the reader the first instant the character appears in the book. Don't write lengthy plot-stopping paragraphs that some readers will be tempted to ignore. Remember the words of the immortal Elmore Leonard and leave out the parts readers skip. Instead, consider which of those details truly need to be conveyed to bring this character to life…and which are just filler. Cut out the filler. And sprinkle the rest of the details throughout the first chapter. The reader absorption rate will be much higher.

If the detail doesn't tell the reader something important about the character, don't bother. Characters will not fail just because the author doesn't give the reader their eye color. The reader will simply supply whatever details they need to imagine the character. That's not a bad thing.

One of the principal reasons people still read, why many people still prefer books to other story-delivering devices, is that they leave room for the imagination. In the astonishingly successful *Twilight* young adult novels, the lead character, Bella, is famously under-described. Did that cause her to be poorly realized in the minds of twenty million or so readers? Far from it. This allowed many female readers to envision themselves as the heroine of the adventure, regardless of their height or hair color, and that contributed to the book's tremendous success. Just make sure the details you do provide create the image you want and lead to the understanding of your character you want the reader to have.

The clever and ingenious writer John Barth once wrote a short story that is actually a writing lesson disguised as fiction. In "Lost in the Funhouse," Barth writes, "The brown hair on Ambrose's mother's forearms gleamed in the sun like."

No, I didn't leave anything out. That's it. In other words, Barth is not going to waste your time inserting a random descriptive simile. If it doesn't matter, he's leaving it out. Supply your own and proceed with the story.

Focus your authorial energy on supplying details that matter because they add up to the character you want to create. The metaphor you're shaping.

An Exercise in Characterization

I hope the purists will forgive me if just this once I turn to the movies for an example, but I think it may be instructive. In fiction, we rarely have an opportunity to see multiple authors interpreting the same character, but in the film world, it happens all the time.

CREATING CHARACTER

Take for instance one of the aforementioned most successful fictional characters of all time, James Bond. As originally created by Ian Fleming, he was a dark and multi-dimensional character, much more so than many of the film adaptations have allowed. Ironically, Fleming chose the name James Bond because he thought it so bland. His point was that most spy work is boring and all Bond's affectations about food and drink and clothes were a cover for how dull he really was. According to Fleming, Bond grew up primarily in Scotland and lost his parents to a climbing accident when he was eleven. The poor orphan was tossed out of Eton for an indiscretion involving a maid, then educated at a lesser school in Edinburgh. He's a man of humble origins, a bachelor, and lonely. All that pseudo-sophisticated pretentiousness about booze and art is the poor Scots kid putting on a show, trying to seem like something he's not.

Sean Connery did not play the character that way. So far as we can tell from any of his films, Sean's Bond was exactly what he appeared to be: an upper crust snob in Saville Row suits, rattling on about champagne while dismissing the Beatles as unbearable noise (see *Goldfinger*). Later generations might think the "vodka martini, shaken not stirred" a rather prissy drink for this cold-hearted macho superspy, but at the time, it was supposed to evidence his sophistication and savoir-faire. The clothes, the drink, the insouciant manner were all bits of characterization suggesting that Bond was exactly what he appeared to be: a tough, heartless spy with refined tastes and a first-rate education.

Roger Moore's character also bore the name James Bond, but he was an entirely different person, and from the first of his films, *Live and Let Die*, he used characterization to put that across. In later years, it became trendy to consider Moore a more light-hearted Bond, but it was not originally so. By the time of *Diamonds Are Forever*, the Connery films had become extremely comic, almost camp. *Live and Let Die* plays it much straighter. As he discusses in his autobiographical tome, *Bond on Bond*, Moore knew that if he imitated Connery, his interpretation would fail. So he created his own Bond, which is why you never saw Moore drive an Aston-Martin and you never heard him order a vodka martini. In that first film, when Moore first enters a bar, he orders, "Bourbon. No ice." Audiences gasped. Because they realized the dude ordering bourbon neat was a far cry from the refined bloke in the white dinner jacket sipping his martini.

Fast forward to the modern era. Inspired by the success of the *Bourne* films, Daniel Craig played a much grittier, more complex character, more like the "blunt instrument" described by Fleming. Craig used none of the pretentious references to food and sometimes drinks straight from the bottle. He occasionally wore a tuxedo but looks uncomfortable in it. *Skyfall* was heralded by some as the best Bond ever—and I think that's because it was the first Bond film in which the character seems to undergo an actual character arc (see the discussion of arc later in this book). *Skyfall* was also the first film to make reference to Bond's troubled childhood. In Craig's first film, an adaptation of *Casino Royale*, he has a hair-raising near-death struggle with poison in the parking lot of the casino, barely resuscitating himself in time. He staggers back into the casino and orders a martini. The bartender asks if he'd like that shaken or stirred, and Craig snaps, "Do I look like I care?"

CREATING CHARACTER

Need I say the obvious? This character may bear the same name, but he is a far cry from the Connery Bond with the Saville Row dinner jacket under his scuba suit. And these different characters were conveyed to the audience, not by telling, but through characterization. They brought these different characters to life through a skillful and careful selection of informative details. And so should you.

WILLIAM BERNHARDT

Highlights

1) Characterization is the observable details. Character is who they really are.

2) Characterization should provide insight into who the character really is.

3) Don't waste your reader's time with characterization that does not provide insight into who the character is.

Red Sneaker Exercises

1) In the last chapter, you developed a metaphor, that is, you considered what your main character represents. Now consider how you're going to suggest this metaphor to the reader. How will you show the reader who this character is at his or her core? As a first step, make a list of five salient traits that define this person's character.

2) Now consider how you will employ characterization to show (without telling) these traits to the reader. For each trait, list three bits of characterization that could inform the reader that the character possesses this trait. For instance, if your character represents the triumph of courage over cowardice, you may decide your character should display a certain fear—because true courage is not about being brave, it's about doing what you need to do even though you're afraid. So for characterization purposes, you will show the character doing something they dislike or fear for a good cause or reason.

38

3) Now look back at the outline you developed (when you read the Red Sneaker book on Structure, perhaps) and consider when you will reveal these key bits of characterization. Don't drop them all into the same scene.

CHAPTER 4: CHARACTER IS CHOICE

Talent is a gift, but character is a choice.
John C. Maxwell

Stories are about conflict. Whether you're writing a short story or a multi-volume generational saga, you must have conflict. That's what keeps the pages turning. That's what maintains the reader's interest. Fundamentally, there must be something the protagonist wants and something or someone that prevents her from obtaining it. What sound is to music, conflict is to story.

In the book on Structure, I wrote that every scene in your book should contain: Event—Change—Conflict. In other words, every scene should portray an event that leads to a change in the protagonist's situation as a result of conflict.

Why are we so obsessed with seeing our protagonists endure hardship? Why must we torture them so? Why do we force them to make all these tough choices?

That how readers find out who they really are.

Character is revealed by choices made under pressure.

Putting Your Characters Under the Knife

In this respect, learning about characters is much like learning about people in real life. We've all encountered the fair-weather friend who is perfectly amiable when performing normal quotidian tasks but completely crumbles at the first sign of trouble. I'm hoping your protagonist has more substance that that. We tend to admire people who undergo hardship and survive, or even prevail. We tend to pity—but not necessarily admire—people who undergo hardship and fail. And we tend to have little patience for people who undergo hardship and whine about it. We like tough, stoic, and resilient heroes. Wah-babies are tiresome—even when they have something legitimate to whine about. In American life and media, we root for underdogs, people with much to overcome but who nonetheless come out ahead…until they become too successful. Then we like to watch them fall. But that's another story.

While you're contemplating the enormous misery you can put your protagonist through, let me remind you that there is a large difference being suffering and surviving. Suffering is not conflict. Watching someone suffer is uncomfortable and ultimately off-putting. While you might be sympathetic, you will eventually tire of the whining and wish the character would take aggressive action to improve their situation. Reading a first-person narrator's endless whining is static, not dynamic, and likely to become tedious quickly. Remember, when readers choose a book, they are in part choosing a character with whom they want to spend a great deal of time. How much time do you want to spend with a hand-wringing wussy? When a more dynamic character is only a whispersync away?

You create problems for your protagonist so that character may be revealed—but you must also make sure that the correct character is revealed. Which does not mean that the character must be perfect. But it probably does meant that they cannot be so completely repellent that people tire of the book.

A famous aphorism often attributed to Aristotle is: "Action is character," which I take to mean that a character's inner self is revealed by their deeds, by what they say and do, rather than by what the author tells you about them. More recently, Chekhov wrote, "Be sure not to discuss your hero's state of mind. Make it clear from his actions." This makes sense. As we all know, talk is cheap. Internal monologue is even cheaper. You get the truth about someone when their thumbs are being screwed. When a character is under pressure, that's when you start to see what they're really made of, to ever-increasing degrees.

The greater the pressure, the deeper the revelation.

This also makes sense. If we gain insight about a character's inner self when they are put under pressure, then even greater pressure should be even more revelatory. A smart aleck might be able to laugh her way through the first few rounds of trouble—but not when the boat begins to sink. The stoic square-jawed hero might be able to maintain his sangfroid through the first few battalions—but not when the enemy kidnaps his mother. Or his pregnant wife. Eventually, something's gotta give. Which is one reason you keep throwing all this horrible stuff at your characters. To some extent, revealing character is like peeling layers from the proverbial onion. Fortunately, since you want the situation to get much worse before it gets better, you will have ample opportunities to reveal everything there is to know about your character.

Characters should undergo increasingly difficult pressures resulting in increasingly difficult problems that reveal their true natures.

In *The Great Gatsby*, Daisy initially has no trouble telling her husband that she doesn't love him and she's running off with Gatsby. After she hits and kills someone while driving, however, everything changes. When serious pressure is applied, we learn the truth about Daisy. First she allows Gatsby to claim he was driving, even though he wasn't. (His behavior under pressure also gives us insight into his elusive character.) She returns home and retreats to the safety of her marriage, allowing Gatsby to take the fall, which of course leads to his doom. Daisy may at first have seemed to be a charming, passionate Southern belle, but when the going gets tough, she is revealed to be selfish, cowardly, submissive, and duplicitous.

In the book on Plot, I go into more detail about how these escalating pressures are accomplished. But for now, suffice to say that there are many levels of conflict: the inner conflict most closely associated with the literary novel, the personal conflict most closely associated with the romance or melodrama, and the external conflict most closely associated with the action story. But whatever the conflict may be, it should worsen as the book progresses. As a result, the reader will feel that they get to know the lead character with greater depth and insight.

Special Abilities

Often, in the course of deepening the pressures and forcing the protagonist to cope, the author will reveal not only greater inner depth but special abilities the protagonist possesses that will help her deal with the conflict. These abilities can come in a wide variety of forms, from superpowers to emotional empathy. This revelation can be equally interesting and equally informative.

CREATING CHARACTER

I don't need to tell you that James Bond has many special abilities, but they all basically come down to a firm resolve and keeping his nerve under pressure, an emotional coolness that may well stem from his upbringing. In other words, these skills are extremely useful in his adventures, but they also tell us something about the character. In *The Hunger Games*, Katniss's archery skills prove useful as she must fight to survive in her world's bizarre variation on bread and circuses. But how did she develop these skills? By sneaking out at night and breaking the law to hunt down food to feed her mother and sister. So again, the skills become important when she is placed under pressure, but they also provide insight into what kind of self-sacrificing person she is.

In the *Twilight* series, for all that Bella might seem a cipher, she has one special ability—an intellectual strength that prevents Edward (a vampire) from being able to read her mind. Ironically, this power draws him to her and deepens their romance. In the blockbuster *Fifty Shades of Grey* trilogy, the heroine Anastasia is eventually revealed to be not only sexually adventurous but also to have innate healing abilities. Her gifts as a healer allow her to ease the psychological torments that plague her lover, Christian Grey, which draws him to her and deepens their romance.

In the best-selling book in the history of mankind, *The Da Vinci Code*, the lead character, Robert Langdon, is a Harvard professor of symbology. Talk about a specialized skill. Microsoft Word doesn't even recognize "symbology" as a word. Langdon is an expert in interpreting signs and symbols. If you hadn't read the book, you might think: So? In 99% of all thrillers, Langdon's skills would be completely useless. But in *The Da Vinci Code*, it's exactly what is needed to follow the trail of breadcrumbs leading to the truth about the Holy Grail, a mystery that has puzzled warriors, kings, and princes for centuries, but is finally unraveled by a Harvard professor.

Is this realistic? In reality, Harvard doesn't even have a department of symbology. Eighty-one million readers didn't care. His skills were useful, and they also give us insight into this somewhat cryptic character who has the love of puzzles and need for historical truth critical to solving this case.

When I set out to write *Dark Eye*, I wanted the lead character, Susan Pulaski, to be everything my better-known protagonist, Ben Kincaid, wasn't. So in terms of external details, she was female, tall, and pushy, as opposed to the male, short, and profoundly introverted Ben. Similarly, she is socially gregarious, sexually aggressive, sharp-tongued, hard-drinking, and at times seemingly arrogant, though that's mostly to cover deep-rooted feelings of inferiority stemming from the loss of her father and her husband. Ben, by contrast, is socially reticent, sexually inhibited, stuttering, virtually teetotalling, and at times too agreeable, though that's mostly to cover the deep intellectual abilities under the surface and perhaps his deep-rooted insecurity stemming from his past damaged relationships... (I know, it all sounds very clinical when you spell it out like that. Another good reason to show rather than tell.)

What about special abilities? Ben may be shy and low-key, but he has a dogged perseverance, a desire to help others, and intellectual gifts that repeatedly help him bring justice to a severely flawed system.

In *Dark Eye* (and the sequel, *Strip Search*), Susan, the psychologist, is paired with Darcy O'Bannon, a young autistic man with extraordinary savant abilities, such as an eidetic memory and phenomenal puzzle-solving abilities. In other words, both he and Susan possess special abilities that, given some other case, might be entirely worthless, but here are invaluable. Susan's insight into the human mind, and particularly aberrant psychology, help her understand this crazed killer drawing his inspiration from literature. Darcy's memory helps him track down the villain's literary clues and his puzzle-solving ability is critical to decoding the multi-tiered cryptograms that the antagonist (like the famed Zodiac Killer) leaves behind. So both Susan and Darcy have special skills that are useful in the story, but also give us insight into their character. Susan's curiosity about the human mind stems from her desire to understand herself and her father. Darcy's need to flaunt his abilities arises from his desire to prove to his father that he is not useless simply because he's autistic.

Some writers rebel when I suggest that they try to instill their characters with memorable powers or abilities. I want my characters to be realistic, they tell me. I'm writing about the real people, the ordinary person struggling with ordinary challenges.

I have two responses to this. First, is it possible that there is something extraordinary in your ordinary person? After all, there must be some reason you feel compelled to write the story. What attracts you to the character? What do you find admirable or noteworthy about them? Do they have an inner strength that keeps them fighting against adversity? Are they particularly sensitive or devoted to the needs of others? Do they approach the day with a zest for living or a winning wit? Perhaps there is something special hiding under all that overt ordinariness. I'm reminded of Judith Guest's heart-wrenching novel *Ordinary People*, involving a troubled teen with an even more troubled mother. Turns out the so-called ordinary people next door are quite extraordinary.

And my second response usually goes something like: Stop being so selfish and start writing a book someone might want to read. No, I don't mean you should pander to the masses or write something you consider garbage. But I also think there's no sense in writing characters with no appeal and then complaining that you can't get your book published. If you want others to read your work, give them a character they will want to read about. You may get points in the faculty lounge for writing "realistic" characters who are humdrum, passive, stupid, or dull, but don't cry on my shoulder when the book isn't widely appreciated. Here's the bottom line: Your book is not going to capture reader's imagination unless there is something out of the ordinary about the characters and their story.

Zeroing In on Your Character

You have four primary tools in any given scene for bringing your character to life: action, appearance, speech, and thought. Use these four in concert with one another, like a conductor orchestrating a symphony. They will reinforce one another, and so long as you have all four in play, you need never descend to showing. Each time you finish a scene, ask yourself if you have used all four to illuminate the main character or characters. If you haven't, add something. If you've resorted to showing, delete it and use one of these four elements instead.

We've already discussed how action can inform character. Appearance is a function of characterization that you use to reveal character. Speech can reveal character not only in terms of the content of the dialogue, but also in terms of how the character communicates what they want the other characters to hear. Stuttering and hesitation are obvious signs of mental state, but there are other subtler possibilities. The use or repetition of a certain phrase. The speed or force of the statement. And you can use internal monologue—sparingly—to let the reader know what is going on in your character's head. Use all four elements and you will see your three-dimensional character springing to life right before your eyes, and the eyes of your readers.

Does your protagonist have any special qualities or abilities? If so, how will they be used in the course of the story, especially when the pressure is on? And even more importantly, how do they give the reader additional insight into the character, so they can understand this character without having exposition or narrative intrusion shoved down their throats?

Highlights

1) Character is revealed by choices made under pressure.

2) The greater the pressure, the deeper the revelation.

3) Characters should undergo increasingly difficult pressures resulting in increasingly difficult problems that reveal their true natures.

4) Special traits and abilities can make your characters more appealing while also giving the reader additional insight into who they really are.

5) Larger-than-life characters delight readers because they do, say, and grow in ways that we cannot.

6) Your book is not going to capture a reader's imagination unless there is something out of the ordinary about the characters and their story.

Red Sneaker Exercises

1) Identify the central conflict of your book, something that occurs early on and sets the plot into motion. Now identify five moments when that conflict escalates, that is, when the pressure on your character increases. How will your character respond to each of these escalations? How will that give the reader additional information about the character?

CREATING CHARACTER

2) Does your protagonist have any special abilities or uncommon traits? If not, can you add some? Look for something that will not only be useful in overcoming adversity during the story, but will also give the reader insight into the character, perhaps because of how the character obtained the ability or why the trait is dominant.

CHAPTER 5: CHARACTER AND CONTRADICTION

I think...if it is true that there are as many minds as there are heads, then there are as many kinds of love as there are hearts.

Leo Tolstoy, Anna Karenina

Creating vivid characters that readers remember is a combination of what you put into the mix and how you write it. This should come as no surprise. Many a book with ordinary characters was made extraordinary by the quality of the writing. Similarly, many books with fairly pedestrian writing were made extraordinary by singular or unique characters (as in many of the bestsellers discussed in this book). To do the best job possible with your characters, you must combine insight, imagination, and first-rate writing skills.

In some of the previous chapters, I focused on stylistic approaches that enhance the vividness of your characters, like showing rather than telling and letting character be revealed through a character's words and deeds rather than narrative intrusion. Beginning in this chapter, I will focus on what you put into the mix, that is, approaches to the actual creation of your characters that will make them more interesting to readers. And the first and perhaps most important of these pertains to the notion of contradiction.

Contradiction, internal or external, makes characters more interesting.

The Three-Dimensional Character

Too often, an early writer will attempt to create characters who are simply too much of a good thing. That is, the protagonists will be infused with positive characteristics and the antagonists will be infused with negative characteristics. In part, this may stem from the previously mentioned tendency for writers to base protagonists upon themselves, coupled with an unfortunate inability to see their own shortcomings, or the desire to pillory a real-life adversary by making them a fictional villain. The better approach is to create characters that are ideal for the story you want to tell, and then to build them from the ground up, making them just as diverse and complex as the most interesting people always are.

Here in the real world, few people if any are all good or all bad. As Emerson famously wrote, "I am large; I contain multitudes." So should your characters. They may have one or two aspects or traits that dominate. But characters that are all good are likely to be hard to take, much less empathize with. Similarly, characters that are all bad may come off as stereotypical and paper-thin. In real life, even the people who committed some of the most heinous atrocities imaginable (think Pearl Harbor, World Trade Center) thought they were good guys. If our world can be populated with people so amazingly diverse and contradictory, why can't your novels? These contradictions, internal or external, are what make characters three-dimensional.

CREATING CHARACTER

When I use the phrase "internal contradictions," I'm essentially referring to characters that are conflicted, at war with themselves, who have internal and perhaps inherent battlegrounds within. Sometimes this is a dichotomy between what characters appear to be and what they really are. Other times it is a dichotomy between what characters want to be and what they are. Or it may be a character tugged in so many different directions he doesn't know what he wants to be or do. This internal conflict will not only make characters interesting to observe, but can also inject major tension into your book. Who can stop reading when a character is thinking, "I don't want to do this—but I must." Or "I know this is wrong and will lead to horrible consequences, but I have to do it anyway." Or even, "I don't know which course to take, but time is running out." This internal tension can make for riveting reading.

The classic example of a conflicted character is Hamlet. If a well-drawn character is three-dimensional, then Hamlet must be about forty-seven-dimensional. He is literally pulled in so many directions he doesn't know what to do next...until his hand is finally forced. He wants to avenge his father's death, but how can he be sure the Ghost told true? He wants to save his mother's honor, but what if Claudius has been falsely accused? He wants revenge, but not while Claudius is praying, because then the man would go straight to heaven and Hamlet would be doing the fiend a favor. Hamlet is so conflicted that he contemplates suicide—"not to be"—rather than "suffering the slings and arrows of outrageous fortune." Might it be better, he wonders, to just "end the heartache and the thousand natural shocks that flesh is heir to?" Hamlet is a revenge play with no real revenge and a thriller with few thrills till the last act—but the entire play is riveting because of the intellectual conflict within Hamlet's mind.

External contradiction comes from pairing two (or more) characters together who are completely different from one another in ways that will make for interesting reading. The unexpected, unusual, or unlikely pairing of opposite types—Mutt and Jeffs, if you're old enough to know what that means—can increase both the humor and the drama. In *Don Quixote*, the title character and his sidekick, Sancho Panza, could not be more different. Quixote is tall and lean, while Panza is short and round. Quixote is a romantic idealist, while Panza is practical and worldwise. In real life, this might make them unable to live with one another, but in the two volumes of this masterpiece, it makes two characters who can take turns supplying what the other needs.

You may have noticed that in any so-called "buddy movie," the buddies are never two guys who are just alike. Much better to pair two completely disparate personalities. In the seminal film in this genre, *48 Hrs.*, the supposedly strait-laced, by-the-book cop Nick Nolte is paired with the rebellious, daring, and completely criminal Eddie Murphy. *Midnight Run* has a similar pairing. And *Planes, Trains and Automobiles*. And *Down and Out in Beverly Hills* (rich man paired with homeless man). And even a film as critically acclaimed as *Schindler's List*. Yes, it's about the Holocaust, but at its heart, the story is driven by two very different men who work together to achieve a common goal. Liam Neeson is Schindler, the German munitions magnate during WWII, and Ben Kingsley is his Jewish accountant. Together they manage to save hundreds of Jews. Stephen Spielberg has said publicly that he had the rights to Thomas Kennealy's marvelous book for years before he made the film because he couldn't figure out how to make it work as a movie. And then he got it: "It's a buddy movie."

In the book that I mentioned earlier, *Dark Eye*, Susan and Darcy could not be more different from one another. Susan is a headstrong, hard-drinking, aggressive, in-your-face psychologist, reeling from horrific blows to her ego and her heart. Darcy is a timid, abstemious, nervous, autistic savant, trying to prove his worth to a father who has given up hoping his boy can lead a normal life. Their profound differences are what makes it endearing to watch them learn to work together, each supplying what the other cannot, essentially completing one another. In the Ben Kincaid books, a similar dichotomy has been in play since the first book in the series. Ben is intelligent, well educated, and idealistic, but reserved and lacking any real social skills. Christina is street-smart, practical, social, and unwilling to take any guff from anyone. This pairing of opposites has worked well for the series.

The Final Resolution

You might be wondering how you're supposed to come up with these marvelously dichotomous characters, especially since I've forbidden you to base them on other people and deride those who base characters upon themselves. I'm trying to prevent you from limiting yourself, or taking the easy way to character, instead of giving it more thought and coming up with something better. For instance, while you do not need to make your protagonist your clone, you might still be able to draw on your own emotional experiences. He doesn't need to look like you, talk like you, have your job, or live in your hometown, but there's no reason why he can't feel some of the same heartache you've known, the disappointment, or the rapture.

The truth is, we are all more diverse than we realize. We really are multitudes, and that means many characters could be drawn from your emotional core. Anton Chekhov once wrote, "Everything I know about human nature I learned from me." You may perceive this as either egomaniac or ingenious. The truth is somewhere in between. Or perhaps a bit of both. We're all so complex and diverse that many true characters could spring from within. This also explains why, if you draw your characters well, with precision and dimensionality, you may find others able to relate to them. Because the truth is, we are all much more alike than we are different.

Let me reference *Dark Eye* one more time. There are three primary characters: Susan Pulaski, the psychologist, Darcy O'Bannon, the autistic savant, and the antagonist, who is killing innocent women in sadistic recreations of scenes from the work of Edgar Allan Poe. We'll call him Edgar (not really his name). Are any of them based upon me? Well, they're certainly not clones. I'm not now nor have I ever been a police psychologist. I'm not autistic. And although you may be wondering at this point, I've never killed anyone, sadistically or otherwise.

But can I relate to these characters? Can I draw anything from within myself to make them come to life? I thought I could. I'm not a psychologist (though I could research my way to a pretty good imitation), but I can relate to Susan's loneliness, her heartache, her awareness that she's making mistakes. And that emotional understanding is far more critical to the character than her educational background.

Similarly, I'm not autistic, but someone close to me is, and I've spent years working and dealing with this particular strain of neurodiversity. I understand the condition at least as well as anybody, but perhaps more importantly, I understand the longing to prove yourself to someone who will probably never be convinced no matter what you do.

You're wondering now if I'm going to compare myself to the killer, right? Well, why not? He is an English major, after all. Has a graduate degree in the field and taught it, just like me. He's just read too darn many books and it's warped his mind. (Kidding. Sort of.) Edgar suffered a particularly vile form of early sexual abuse, as did most serial killers. That idea came from research, not experience. But what does Edgar want? Why does he do these terrible things? Because he's convinced himself, based upon a twisted reading of Poe's strange cosmological work, *Eureka*, that recreating these gruesome death scenes will somehow open a passageway to Dreamland, Poe's paradise. He doesn't want to hurt anyone. He just wants to escape this horrible world filled with the slings and arrows of outrageous fortune and to take us all to a more peaceful place. He's Hamlet, in other words, except all the internal conflict eventually drives him completely mad (as indeed some readers believe Hamlet is). So no, Edgar is not me, but I get it. I get the desperation to find a better, kinder place free from backstabbing and cruelty and greed. Who doesn't?

Since I mentioned that some form of child abuse lay in Edgar's past, let me take a moment to caution you against creating dark characters who are completely explained in the latter portions of the book by some horrific childhood incident. This has been overdone, sometimes by fine writers, to such an extent that it has become a tired cliché. Try to avoid the temptation to reduce your characters to a single tragic event. Most people are considerably more complex. I don't know where this instinct comes from. Perhaps from *Citizen Kane*, often called the most important film ever made—but let's remember that it earned that title with its inventive camerawork, not from the complexity of its screenplay, too mired in trendy 1930s-Freudianism for my taste. So it turns out that all he really wants is to be an innocent widdle boy again playing with his sled before they took him from his mommy. Give me a break.

I hope this discussion is making two points clear. If you want to invest your characters with emotional truth, you must be willing to explore your own experiences, emotional and otherwise, not so you can create clone-characters, but so you can create characters with real feelings and emotions, grappling with the traumas and challenges with which we all must deal. And the second is that you must also pay attention to the world around you, to learn about people who are different from you. Writers are the packrats of the universe. Writers are people who listen far more than they talk. Writers are people who don't hear what their companions told them in a restaurant because they were eavesdropping on the conversation at the table behind them. You never know what might be useful, which is why you should always be absorbing. Many a time I've been writing and suddenly recalled an incident or conversation from many years before that was exactly what I needed at that moment in my book. Good thing I'm blessed with a sturdy memory.

Of course, once you become known for this sort of thing, you will find that in the middle of relating an anecdote, your friends stop and say, "Is this going to be in one of your books?"

And the honest answer, of course, is, "I don't know yet. Is it any good?"

Sometimes One Dimension is Enough

While we're considering approaches to creating three-dimensional characters, I should make another point.

Not all characters should be three-dimensional.

Was your first reaction to this statement horror and dismay? Were you appalled that I had the audacity, not only to say it, but to put it in boldface? I hope not. I've already said that your finished novels will likely have dozens of characters. If you stop to describe and give extended expository background information on all of them your book will be long and dull indeed. So in a sense, this is simply reiterating a previous idea, but doing it in the context of character dimensionality. I've said that complexity and contradiction can make a character more interesting. But you should also understand that there are some instances when a character can survive with less complexity, and may be better off without it.

You've read my admonition that antagonists are more interesting when they are not painted all black. On the other hand, my friend Grant Blackwood has argued long and persuasively that, for the adventure novels that he writes, less complex villains are better, because readers want a confrontation between good and evil, not a long digression into what ails the human soul or whether his father ever said "I love you." The important distinction perhaps is not between one-dimensional and three-dimensional, but between one-dimensional and cardboard.

In some instances, one dimension is enough—if that dimension is sufficiently interesting to engage the reader and propel the plot forward.

Since I discussed Shakespeare's longest tragedy in the previous section, let's discuss his shortest here. I've heard people argue that the lead characters in *Macbeth*—which would be Macbeth and Lady Macbeth—are one-dimensional characters, both driven by ambition to extreme acts. I don't agree, but I understand the argument, and even if it is true, it doesn't undermine the play at all. Initially, Macbeth may be driven by ambition, but he comes to despair of his decision to kill Duncan to such an extent that he sees all life as futile and useless, "a tale told by an idiot, full of sound and fury, signifying nothing." Even if he didn't start with many dimensions, he gains them by the end. Similarly, Lady Macbeth may be defined initially by her pushy ambitions, but she too is so overwhelmed by remorse that she ends up sleepwalking and wringing imaginary blood out of her hands. Even if these characters are essentially one-dimensional, they are far from boring (and given the brevity of the play, it is entirely possible that added scenes, deepening the characters, have been lost).

Much has been written about Dan Brown's villains—the albino killer monk in *The Da Vinci Code*, the somewhat similar tattooed genius in *The Lost Symbol*—and not all of it has been complimentary. But I note that even in these fast-paced thrillers, he takes the time to create plausible background stories and motivations. By the end of *Code*, you find yourself actually sympathizing with this poor manipulated murderous monk. These characters may not be multi-dimensional, but they seem real, credibly motivated, and even permit empathy. To me, that's good writing.

CREATING CHARACTER

In most horror stories, and virtually all horror movies, the antagonist, i.e., the monster, is one-dimensional. He's a monster. (The Frankenstein Creature is a notable exception, but that's largely because he came from an exceptionally excellent book.) It's not terribly important to know the monster's motivation. It just needs to terrify. In my favorite, *Jaws*, I don't think you could call the antagonist—the shark—a complex character. He's a swimming killing machine. That's it. And that's more than enough. Similarly, James Cameron's science fiction adventure *The Terminator* is a terrific movie, but the Arnold Schwarzenegger title character is not what I would call multi-layered. He wants to kill Sarah Conner, and he's willing to do whatever it takes to make that happen. Deep? No. Effective? Incredibly.

Of course, the other main characters in these works—Dr. Frankenstein, Sarah Conner, Sheriff Brody—are more complex. Some major character in your story needs to be multi-dimensional. But not everyone.

Highlights

1) Contradiction, internal or external, makes characters more interesting. This is the fundamental quality found in three-dimensional characters.

2) Not all characters need to be three-dimensional.

Red Sneaker Exercises

1) Previously, you came up with five words that define your main characters. Are they all one-dimensional, that is, all good or all bad? If so, see if you can make your characters more complex. Add a bad trait to the good guys and a good trait to the bad guys.

2) Now see if you can inject some contradictory characteristics, such as self-doubt, agenda conflict, or mutually exclusive goals. Can you make it worse? Can you make the inward conflict seem irreconcilable?

3) Who are your two primary lead characters (excluding antagonists)? Perhaps the protagonist and a best friend or sidekick? Compare and contrast them. Are they more alike or more different? How can you sharpen the distinctions between them, preferably in a way that leads to drama or humor? Do they like or admire one another?

4) Think about the best and worst experiences you've ever had. What emotions did you feel? Why? How can you plumb those emotional experiences and inject them into your characters?

5) Can you sympathize with all your characters (even the bad ones)? In other words, do you understand what they do and why they do it?

CHAPTER 6: CONSIDERING THE PROTAGONIST

Perfect heroines, like perfect heroes, aren't relatable, and if you can't put yourself in the protagonist's shoes, not only will they not inspire you, the book will be pretty boring.

Cassandra Clare

Without question, the most important character in your novel is the protagonist, the main character, the one whose journey shapes the book. At some level, or for some reason, the reader must want to spend time with this character. That does not mean the character must be a saint, or even likable. That does not mean readers must emphasize with the character or have similar experiences in their past. There are few absolutes here, except that the reader must look forward to spending time with this character. And here's another absolute: The protagonist cannot be boring. If your lead is dull, your book is doomed.

Sometimes early writers will ask if their book can have more than one protagonist. The answer I usually give is some variation of "It depends," but a more helpful answer would probably be: "No." Sure, it can be done, and anyone with an English degree can conjure up an example from the past. But for the most part, readers enjoy the experience of seeing the story unfold through the viewpoint of a central character, of seeing what they see, learning what they learn, and vicariously doing what they do. This does not mean you cannot have multiple viewpoints (see the later discussion of viewpoint) or that you can't have more than one important character. But the reader needs to feel grounded, and that comes from a subconscious understanding that the tale being told is essentially the protagonist's story.

Given the wide variety of books and protagonists arising in the four hundred year history of the novel, you might imagine there are no rules. Well perhaps, but to paraphrase a great pirate, there are certainly guidelines, which can only be disregarded at your book's peril. Let me see if I can summarize the rules for protagonists in one sentence.

The protagonist must have a goal or desire, a chance to obtain it, and something that makes him/her/it appealing to the reader.

The Object of Desire

John D. McDonald once famously defined story as, "Stuff happens to people you care about." That's pretty darn good and admirably concise. I once heard my friend William Martin define story even better: "There must be something your protagonist wants, and someone or something preventing him from getting it." That's conflict in a nutshell, and understanding is a good starting point for creating your protagonist.

There must be something your protagonist wants. In an action-adventure novel or thriller, this may be obvious. In William Martin's *The Lincoln Letter*, Peter Fallon must find Abraham Lincoln's diary. In Steve Berry's *The*

CREATING CHARACTER

Alexandria Link, Cotton Malone must save his son. In John Lescroart's Dismas Hardy books, the distinguished attorney must save his client. Indiana Jones seeks the Lost Ark of the Covenant. In a romance novel, the protagonist seeks a loving relationship. In a mystery, the detective seeks an answer. In a literary novel, typically, the protagonist seeks some inner goal, such as harmony, or maturity, or truth. Regardless of what you're writing, your protagonist must want something. The protagonist's journey or quest for that goal is what drives the novel forward—and what keeps the reader turning the pages.

Possibly, the protagonist does not know what he or she wants initially, or perhaps what they really want isn't what they think or what they say. Or what they want turns out to be something other than what the protagonist expects. That's fine. In fact, that might lead to some amazing plot twists or revelations later in the book. But the protagonist still must have a reason to get out of bed, so to speak, even if the reason is completely wrongheaded.

Voltaire's Candide starts his comic journey, aided by Dr. Pangloss (a sidekick distinctly different from the lead character) searching for philosophical truth and the answers to great questions, such as "Is this the best of all possible worlds?" What he finds is (depending upon how you read the last sentence) something of more practical value. In *The Da Vinci Code*, Robert Langdon starts his quest for the Holy Grail thinking he's looking for a cup. The Grail turns out to be something much more interesting. Far from disappointing readers, this makes the story a thousand times more engaging. What matters is that at every step of the story, there is something these characters want. All their actions are in pursuit of that goal.

69

The protagonist also must have some chance of obtaining that goal. I hope this is obvious to you, but I've read a few manuscripts in which protagonists sought some "Impossible Dream," only to be inevitably disappointed. This rarely leads to a satisfying book. (If you're thinking *Don Quixote* is an example, it isn't. Go read the book.) Mind you, the odds may be terrifically stacked against the protagonist—in thrillers, they usually are. But the protagonist must not appear to be a fool wasting his time. Who would want to read that book? I'm not saying that the protagonist must always succeed, either. But there must seem to be a chance, however remote.

In the previous chapter, we discussed the possibility of endowing your character with special powers or abilities. Those abilities may ultimately explain why your character succeeds even though the obstacles seem insurmountable. No one knew your character could do what she does. Maybe not even the protagonist herself. But when your protagonist uses her ability to accomplish the goal, that provides a satisfying way of snatching an almost impossible victory from what previously seemed hopeless.

Appealing Protagonists

The third, and by far most critical of the requirements contained in this definition pertains to appeal. At some level, or for some reason, the protagonist must be appealing. This doesn't mean they must be sexy, pretty, kind, generous, brave, trustworthy or reverent. It simply means they must appeal to the reader for some reason, which is essentially another way of saying they must interest the reader. They must cause the reader to want to read about their journey.

CREATING CHARACTER

I think character appeal can be broken down into two categories.

Your protagonist either must be sympathetic or empathetic.

What's the difference? If readers are going to sympathize with your characters, they must be likable. Which fortunately does not require perfection. Think back upon your own life and see if there aren't people you've liked for odd reasons, or despite flaws, or even though they didn't deserve it. And if you can't make your character likeable, consider whether you can make your character empathetic. By that, I don't mean that the protagonist empathizes with others. I mean that the reader can empathize with the protagonist and her struggle. In other words, there must be something that protagonist has or has been through that the reader can relate to.

One of the most popular characters to arise in recent years is Thomas Harris's Dr. Hannibal Lecter. At this point, I don't think the popularity can be denied. Lecter has been featured in at least four films, three books, and two television series. And this character's popularity comes despite the fact that he is—well, how can I put this nicely? A cannibal. Hannibal the Cannibal kills people in strange and grotesque ways, then eats them. And yet people love reading about this character. Why? How can anyone find this horrible man appealing?

Well, he is rather charming. He's smart, well-educated, and has a great deal of flair. Erudite, sophisticated. Knowledgeable about art and wine. In many respects, he is similar to James Bond, who also kills repeatedly, though to my knowledge he has never dined on his victims. You can't even call Hannibal heartless. Although he taunts Clarisse throughout *The Silence of the*

Lambs, he also shows her considerable sympathy and affection. After he escapes FBI custody, he assures her, "I'm not coming for you." In the follow-up book, *Hannibal*, his affection for Clarisse is even more pronounced. Her employers are not her friends—they toss her out for one alleged error in judgment. Hannibal is the one who befriends her and wants to take care of her. Granted, his plans for drawing her into his world are completely twisted, but what did you expect?

My point is that Hannibal Lecter is about as non-empathetic as it is possible for a character to be. There is no way that anyone could relate to him personally (I hope). But is he likeable? Yes. Perversely so, but yes.

Let's reconsider Macbeth, another notorious lead character, who is, though not a cannibal, certainly a murderer. Worse, he commits regicide, considered in his time one of the most heinous crimes imaginable. You may or may not find him sympathetic. He lets his wife and his ambition drive him to unspeakable acts. But can you empathize with him? I certainly can. Who amongst us has never made a mistake? We've all made mistakes, and even if we've never made one so titanic as regicide, we can still empathize with the guilt and remorse of someone who has let his vanity or ambition cloud his thinking. In this imperfect world, Macbeth is everyman.

Sometimes early writers will want to create a character so dark or flawed that likeability becomes a problem. Typical examples are characters battling depression, bipolar disorder, alcoholism, drug abuse, gambling, sex addiction, and so forth. One possible solution is to make the character aware that they have a problem—and struggle to remedy it. While we may not admire their flaws, we can empathize with the battle to overcome the problem.

To quote George R. R. Martin, "Many roads lead to the same castle." There are many ways to create characters, but when the path has been crossed and the book has been written, if the reader cannot form a bond with your protagonist, your book will not capture their imagination. So in the next chapter, we will discuss how to make your characters more likeable—despite their flaws.

The Bad Guy

Before we move on, let's consider the other important character in your book, the antagonist. Do I have a definition detailing the requirements for the antagonist? As a matter of fact, I do.

The antagonist must have a goal or desire, a chance to obtain it, and something that makes him/her/it appealing to the reader.

Sound familiar? Creating a dynamic, engaging antagonist should be no different from creating your protagonist, except perhaps in scope. After all, if your protagonist's opposition is uninteresting, how much fun can it be to watch them battle one another? Your antagonist must also want something, something that puts him in direct opposition to your protagonist. Your antagonist must have some chance of success, or there is no suspense. And yes, on some level or in some way, the antagonist must be appealing, which means they must be either sympathetic or empathetic.

A well-motivated antagonist with understandable, even sympathetic motivations is the difference between creating a memorable opponent and a comic-book baddie.

Although actually, even in comic books, the best villains can still garner sympathy. John Rogers once wrote that, "You don't really understand an antagonist until you understand why he's a protagonist in his own version of the world."

In the original comic-book continuity, Superman caused Lex Luthor to lose his hair. Small wonder he hates the big blue Boy Scout. In later incarnations, Lex was the big man in Metropolis—till Supes hit the scene and stole his thunder, not by being smart or accomplished, but because he has cool powers he didn't earn but are simply an accident of birth. Can you see how that might generate some resentment? The same resentment you may have experienced for the co-worker who was promoted ahead of you based upon looks, or clothes, or family connections?

One of the best-known literary antagonists is Iago, from Shakespeare's *Othello*. Iago is such a miserable little wretch he persuades Othello that his newlywed bride, Desdemona, has been unfaithful. Othello becomes so inflamed with jealousy and rage that the noble Moor ultimately suffocates his entirely innocent wife. How could Iago be such a fiend? Because Iago, like Lex Luthor and many others, has been passed over. Othello promoted another soldier (Cassio), so Iago takes revenge. Racism may also be a factor, since Othello is a dark-skinned man living in predominantly white Venice. You may not empathize with the racism, I hope, but you understand that it has motivated countless horrifying deeds throughout history.

We could hold a long debate over whether Captain Ahab is the protagonist or antagonist of Melville's marvelous *Moby Dick*. For now, let's content ourselves to say he is a flawed and less than perfect character. He is so driven by the need for revenge (against an unthinking beast that probably has little or no awareness of Ahab's existence) that he endangers his own crew and causes many deaths in his pursuit of satisfaction. He commits the unpardonable sin (for a sailing man) of refusing to help a fellow captain search for his lost son—because he's too busy gunning for the whale. Hard to like this guy...until you realize how this whale has ruined his life. Moby Dick took a piece of his leg, and it's not hard to see the emasculation metaphor (not hard with Luthor losing his hair, either). Ahab tells Starbuck he has been "distant" from his wife ever since. The whale has stolen his status not only as a sailor but as a man. Hence, "from hell's gate, I stab at thee."

In *Dark Eye*, the antagonist is the serial killer we've code-named "Edgar" because of his obsession with the works of Edgar Allan Poe. Serial killers have challenged modern writers because they seem to sidestep plausible motivations—the killer is "just plain crazy." My research indicates just the opposite. There are still understandable and perhaps even sympathetic reasons why serial killers do what they do. The difference is that the motivation is not so much about the victim as it is about the killer's tortured past. What I tried to do was create an antagonist who, like Hannibal Lecter, could commit horrific crimes, but could still engender a reader's sympathy, in part because they understood the cesspool from which he emerged, and in part because he means no one ill will. Edgar simply has a misguided notion about how he will take us all to Poe's paradisiacal Dreamland.

In psychoanalytical circles, you sometimes hear the term "agenda conflict," meaning that two opposing people or groups want different things. I think this is a useful way to think about the conflict between your protagonist and antagonist. In other words, stop thinking about the conflict in terms of "good guy" and "bad guy." Instead, think of it as a clash between two people, both part good and part bad but who have conflicting goals. You may find that increases the sophistication level of your characters. Ultimately, of course, you want readers to sympathize more with the protagonist—which will probably happen automatically because we start with the protagonist and see the story unfold through his eyes. But your story will be richer if we see your antagonist as a three-dimensional character with realistic motivations rather than as someone who is simply "evil" or "crazy" or "greedy."

CREATING CHARACTER

Highlights

1) The protagonist must have a goal or desire, a chance to obtain it, and something that makes him/her/it appealing to the reader.

2) Your protagonist must either be sympathetic or empathetic.

3) Protagonists do not have to be flawless to be likeable.

4) The antagonist must have a goal or desire, a chance to obtain it, and something that makes him/her/it appealing to the reader.

5) The best antagonists have strong and understandable motivations for the actions they take in opposition to the protagonist.

Red Sneaker Exercises

1) What is your protagonist's goal or desire? What does he or she want? How does that motivate the journey charted by your book? Does the goal change over the course of the book? Does the goal turn out to be something other than what the character anticipated it would be?

2) What is your protagonist's defining quality? What makes this character stand out from other similarly situated persons?

CHAPTER 7: VIEWPOINT

There is nothing insignificant in the world. It all depends on the point of view.

Johann Wolfgang von Goethe

Viewpoint is not the same as character, though the two are closely related, which is why I've included this discussion in this book. I've placed it after the discussion of your protagonist because that viewpoint is by far the most important one you will write.

Sometimes writers confuse character and viewpoint. They tell me they only have one character in their book—because it's all written from a first-person viewpoint. Or they tell me they have multiple protagonists—because they have multiple viewpoints. The distinction is important because it affects your understanding of your book. And if you don't understand your book, how well could you possible write it?

Viewpoint Never Takes a Vacation

Here is the simplest, most direct thing I can tell you about viewpoint:

You are always writing in someone's viewpoint.

This is not just a metaphysical precept on the nature of writing. This is the truth, and you need to understand that to avoid some really bad writing that will almost certainly prevent you from publishing your work. You must always be in some character's viewpoint as your write your novel. Yes, you may have multiple viewpoints, if you find that useful and advantageous—though the protagonist's viewpoint should always predominate. Readers do not want to feel as if they have been thrown into a fictional world and abandoned, left to wander about with nothing to ground them. They want to experience this world through the eyes of your characters. That's what makes them feel grounded in the story. That's what makes it seem like more than just a series of events. That's what brings it to life.

You may be thinking—wait a minute. I understand that when I write in first, second or third person, I'm writing in the viewpoint of a character. But what about when I'm writing from an omniscient viewpoint?

My first response is: Don't. Really. Don't.

My second response is: You're still writing in a viewpoint. Yours.

Let me explain. Omniscient viewpoint is greatly disfavored in contemporary fiction, disfavored to the extent of being almost unpublishable. Perhaps this disturbs you. Perhaps you're thinking of all those great nineteenth-century novelists who occasionally employed the omniscient voice, Dickens and Hardy and the like. What you need to understand is that the novel is a relatively new art form, only about four hundred years old, and like anything new, it's evolving. Reading tastes evolve, too. And contemporary readers prefer to get their information from a character rather than straight from the author. When they get it through the observations and experiences of a character, they feel immersed in the story. When they get it straight from the author, they feel yanked out of the story. You've broken the fourth wall.

CREATING CHARACTER

Here's the truth, and I hope it doesn't hurt your feelings: When readers read your book, they don't want to think about you. They want to be immersed in the world you've created. After they've finished the book, after they've turned the final page, their eyes filled with tears of joy at the magnificence they have just experienced, then, yes, then they will see your author photo and think, "What a genius this writer is."

But not while they're reading. Omniscient viewpoint takes them out of the story. Which is why it is little used today.

Now, some stories have a narrator. Not the same thing. Books such as *The Notebook* and *Water for Elephants* use the framing device of an elderly character telling the story of what went before. All thirteen volumes of *The Series of Unfortunate Events* are narrated by "Lemony Snicket"—but is he the author? No. He is a fictional character, "The Author," invented by the real author David Handler, to give the stories the arch faux-tragic voice he sought. This is not omniscient viewpoint. These are clever and effective framing devices.

There is no information you can provide through omniscient narration that cannot also be provided through a character's viewpoint. You might have to be clever about it. You might have to bring it out in dialogue or give your viewpoint character a natural reason to be thinking about these facts—preferably not a nightmare, the discovery of an old, yellowed photograph, or a visit from a long-lost grandparent. Infodumps are always disfavored, whether they come from omniscient narrators or anyone else. But when the information comes from something organic to the story, it seems more natural and less intrusive. Readers still will be securely lodged in your fictional universe—which just became a great deal richer.

Sometimes writers, particularly those on the literary side of the fence, want to resort to omniscient narration so they can deploy some lovely turn of phrase or elegant poetic language. Certainly many of the writers of the past did so. "It was the best of times; it was the worst of times." But we live in the twenty-first century, not the nineteenth. While I'm not saying that you can never use lovely language, I will say it is important for the writer not to attract attention to him or herself. You want the reader thinking about the story and the characters, not you. Praise for your use of language may be flattering, but it is less likely to lead to immersive reading. You have perhaps heard the phrase: You have to kill your darlings. This is exactly what it means. If you've got a phrase that stands out so well it makes you smile at your cleverness every time you read it—it probably needs to go. Remember that at the end of the day, your primary goal is to tell a story. The superb writer Robert Harris said, "It is perfectly legitimate to write novels which are essentially prose poems, but in the end, I think, a novel is like a car, and if you buy a car and grow flowers in it, you're forgetting that the car is designed to take you somewhere else."

Let your readers absorb your tale through the eyes and ears of the characters. If you do that and do it well, praise for your work will come—for the right reasons, not the wrong ones.

Psychic Distance

Put as little distance as possible between your reader and your viewpoint character.

CREATING CHARACTER

Some writing instructors distinguish "third person close" from "third person distant," but in recent years, the term "psychic distance" has become more popular, perhaps because it just sounds so darn cool. David Morrell, fabulous thriller writer and former Iowa Writers Workshop instructor, has done much to popularize the term. Whatever you call it, this is a useful tool for skillfully causing your reader to become more deeply entrenched in your viewpoint character's head, which is exactly what you want.

Here's how you do it:

1) Identify the viewpoint character in the first sentence of each new scene.

2) Never use that character's name again throughout the scene. When necessary, refer to that character as "he" or "she" (or "I" if you're in first person). Using the name again draws the reader out of the character's head, leaving the reader feeling like someone looking at the character as an outside observer.

3) To avoid confusion, no other character can be called "he" or "she" (whichever one you're using for the viewpoint character). They must always be identified by name, or by some other identifier, i.e., "the tall man," or "the assailant," or "her mother."

These rules are much easier to announce than to deploy. You probably won't get it entirely right in your first draft, especially if you're doing this for the first time. That's okay. You can fix it in your later drafts, of which there will be many. This becomes particularly tricky in scenes involving many characters of the same gender. The temptation to repeat your viewpoint character's name will be powerful. When they start speaking to one another, you may feel it imperative to identify the viewpoint character by name. Otherwise, how will the reader know who is saying what?

This can be accomplished without repeating the viewpoint character's name, but it requires considerable skill. If you're writing a back-and-forth conversation, an interrogation, or a leader doling out assignments, attribution may be unnecessary. Your goal is to write the dialogue so well that it is clear to the reader who is speaking without being told. And if that just doesn't work for you, as a last resort, have the other party call the viewpoint character by name. "What do you think, Susan?" This is hardly ideal (the book on Dialogue will explain why), but it doesn't pull the reader out of viewpoint, and it's better than allowing your reader to be confused.

Even if you're writing a book entirely told from one viewpoint, it's never a bad idea to reestablish that viewpoint in the first sentence of each scene. And if you're writing in multiple viewpoints, it's imperative. Don't let the reader be lost or confused, not for even a sentence. In Steve Berry's books, he not only identifies the viewpoint character in the first sentence of each scene, he does it in the first *word* of each scene. You may not feel like you have to be that vigorous about it, but you can't question that his approach has been successful and has led to some supremely readable books. Your goal is for your readers to have a smooth ride without speed bumps. When the viewpoint is unclear, readers slow down and become confused, even if they don't know exactly why. Don't let that happen.

If you start a scene in one viewpoint, do you have to remain in that viewpoint for the entire scene? No, though that's the way it typically goes. There may be situations in which you want to start a scene in one viewpoint, then shift to the other character to give the reader insight into their reaction. In that case, you must make a clean break—meaning you insert extra space between paragraphs to demonstrate that one scene has ended and another has begun—even if there has been no change of location or action or characters. Establish the new viewpoint character in the first sentence. Then proceed with the scene. Remember, there are no hard and fast rules in writing, but it is never a good idea to confuse the reader. Intrigue the reader, sure. Questions you've deliberately left unanswered for the time being, great. Mystery keeps readers reading. Confusion does not.

Another question to consider when establishing a close link between your readers and your character is what you want to call the character. Do you call them by their first name, last name, nickname, or something else? There's no rule for this. You need to determine what works best to create the degree of closeness you want. Generally speaking, putting readers on a first-name basis with a character will make them feel closer to the character. On the other hand, if you're writing a thriller, you may feel that only a tough monosyllabic last name gives the character the macho stature you want, i.e., "Bond" or "Pitt." The only rule is that whatever you decide, you must stick to it consistently. Don't confuse the reader by calling the same character by different names.

In the Kincaid series, I have a triumvirate of key characters: Ben, Christina, and Mike. Therefore, I always refer to them as Ben, Christina, and Mike (although on occasion, a third-party might use their last names in conversation). Virtually every other character was known by their last name. On occasion, I allowed a new viewpoint character to be known by their first name, signaling their importance—for instance, a potential love interest for Ben.

So the triumvirate remained closest to the reader, and others were at least slightly more distant, depending upon their relevance to the story.

Finally, let me dispense with this antiquated idea of "first person close" or "third person distant" or whatever. The idea seems to be that for some characters, even though we're in their viewpoint, we don't want the reader to be too close to them—hence, third person distant. So you write from their viewpoint, but never allow any interior monologue, or something like that. This seems completely stupid to me. If you've bothered to take a reader into someone's viewpoint, you've done it for a reason—so we can experience the story through their eyes. Being a little in someone's viewpoint is like being a little pregnant. You either are or you aren't. So don't do a halfway job of it. Remember, just because you're in someone's viewpoint doesn't mean the character is a nice person. The fact that you have multiple viewpoints portrayed well won't diminish the importance of the protagonist. If you have brought your protagonist to life, given them a complex, fully realized personality, not to mention more pages than anyone else, your reader should not be confused about who is the central character.

CREATING CHARACTER

Highlights

1) You are always writing in someone's viewpoint.

2) Put as little distance as possible between your reader and your viewpoint characters.

Red Sneaker Exercises

1) Identify all your viewpoint characters. Now decide how you will refer to them throughout the book— first name, last name, nickname, etc. Strategize about how to make it clear who the most important characters are.

2) Review the first chapter of your work-in-progress. Is the viewpoint character identified in the first sentence? Can you refrain from using that name again in that scene? If this is not the first appearance of your protagonist, look for that scene and see if you can avoid repetitions of the character's name that may draw the reader out of the character's head.

CHAPTER 8: MAKING READERS CARE

I spend many hours in conversation with wonderful characters from fascinating books.

Patti Roberts

Reading is a sacred rite, a form of communion, if you will. It's an intimate relationship between two people who quite possibly have never even met: the reader and the writer. Both of these people enter into a shared world, created by the writer, but nurtured by readers who voluntarily decide to spend their time there. This is communion and conversation, enriching both intellectually and, in the best cases, spiritually.

Now ask yourself this question: How long would you stay in a conversation (much less a communion) with someone you don't like? Seriously. Imagine you're at a party. You meet some new people. You're talking to them, probably also subconsciously sizing them up. If you like them, you might end up spending the rest of the evening with them. (You might even end up taking them back to your place so you can extend the conversation.) If you find them interesting, unique, complex, or even deranged, that might prolong the conversation. But if you just flat out don't like them, find them utterly unappealing, you will most likely say something about how you need to freshen your drink and move on.

Characters are like that, too. There are many ways to cause a reader to like your character. They may be attracted to your protagonist's lively sense of humor, bold courage, loving heart, sense of honor, or strength in the face of adversity. They may be attracted by your protagonist's Machiavellian manipulative skills, brutal efficiency, rebellious anarchic spirit, or sexual deviancy. Like George R.R. Martin said, many paths to the castle.

But if they can't stand your characters, or don't respect them, they will put your book down and start something else. Which means the conversation ends, the spiritual link is severed, and your book will not find its audience.

So how do you make your protagonist likeable?

The most obvious way to make your protagonist likeable is to instill him or her with the virtues that we humans typically admire most. How can we not feel sympathy toward someone who embodies (or is a metaphor for) great attributes? We admire people when we detect honesty, courage, loyalty, kindness, trust, devotion, spirituality, purity, passion, integrity, and love of others. Instilling those qualities in your hero can't help but make him more likeable, though I would avoid using all of them, lest the character be unbearable. One or two will suffice.

It takes time (meaning words) to demonstrate that your character possesses these qualities, especially if you have to show it rather than simply telling. But you need readers to like your main character almost immediately. If the reader is not engaged with your protagonist, they will likely lose interest in his story, sometimes with cruel rapidity. Generally speaking, readers tell me they give a book about five pages to grab them, and if it hasn't by then, they move on to something else. So you have all of five pages—maybe a thousand words—to forge a connection to your reader by demonstrating that your character is honest, brave, kind, etc. Good luck.

Fortunately, there is a quick fix here, a short-term plan to develop character appeal. This is not a substitute for imbuing your protagonist with more meaningful and profound traits. These are ways of attracting reader sympathy in the short term, to keep them reading in those early pages, until you have time to reveal the character's more profound positive attributes. Don't try to use them all. Use in small doses, as necessary.

One warning: The secrets I am about to reveal will likely ruin books, plays, and movies for you till the end of time. Why? Because once I've made you aware of these tricks for engendering reader sympathy, you will start to see them everywhere. You will understand why the thriller hero stops to rescue a cat from a tree. You will understand why the tormented fleeing husband stops to help the elderly woman lift her baggage into the overhead bin. You'll say, "I know why the writer did that!" And you'll feel quite proud for a moment or two. Then you'll realize the story is completely ruined for you.

And then you'll understand why many fiction writers read a lot of nonfiction.

Okay, fine, keep reading. But don't say I didn't warn you.

The Expert

Demonstrate that your protagonist is very good at what he or she does.
The appeal here should be obvious. We admire people who are good at their work. Understandably so.

People who are good at what they do are typically smart, well-educated. We should admire them. That's why so many television programs center around professionals, doctors and lawyers and cops and other people whose jobs involve them in the lives of others in high-stakes scenarios. They may not succeed in each and every case, but it isn't because they aren't capable.

As I mentioned earlier, one of the most successful characters of all time is Sherlock Holmes. Given the fascination readers have shown for this character for over a hundred years, we can assume that he is keenly likeable, right?

Except not. As I discussed before, he's everything but likeable. He's particularly cold toward women (except of course, *the* woman, Irene Adler, who he appears to admire essentially because she's just like him). Holmes is fundamentally what my mother would call, "not a nice person." So how can he be appealing? Why do we go on reading these stories?

Because he's very good at what he does. And he does something no one else can do. He's smart, too, another trait we admire, at least until it makes us feel inferior. But there's no doubt that Holmes is better than anyone else at detecting. He spins circles around Scotland Yard. He solves every case. The only time he even arguably fails is in "A Scandal in Bohemia" (interestingly, the first Holmes short story), but even there, you suspect that letting Irene Adler escape is more a matter of professional courtesy.

You may be familiar with the television series *House*. Did you realize that the character Dr. House is based upon Sherlock Holmes? (Holmes equals House. Get it?) Like Holmes, he's a detective, though his field is medicine rather than crime. He is equally abrasive and misanthropic. He's a drug addict (like the early Holmes). His best friend is Wilson (like Watson). His house number is 221. And if you saw the last episode, you realize he even faked his own death, just as Holmes did in "The Final Problem." (The street in the final scene is named for the Reichenbach Falls, where Holmes supposedly fell to his death.) So given this information, you may be better equipped to answer the question: Why was this show so popular? Why did people enjoy watching this horrible man work?

Because he was very good at what he did. Better than anyone else. No one else came close.

So one way to create appeal for your protagonist is to show that he is extremely good at what he does, perhaps the best. Show it happening. Perhaps have someone else comment upon it. Those James Bond movies started with a larger-than-life action sequence for a reason: to tell you right off the bat how good this man is at the spy game. Nobody does it better.

Can you give your character that level of excellence and expertise? If you do, how can we resist him?

The Clown

Another reliable way to attract readers to your character is to give them a sense of humor.

We like people who make us laugh. Doesn't everyone like to laugh? Every time someone polls people on what qualities they're looking for in a romantic partner, the top answer is always the same: a sense of humor. (To be fair, this may seem more socially correct than identifying an oversized body part.) We may have different triggers. I love PG Wodehouse and Anne Tyler, while someone else may prefer H.L. Mencken and Henry Fielding. I love Charles Chaplin and Woody Allen, while someone else may prefer Buster Keaton and Mel Brooks. But we all love to laugh. So having a character with a sharp sense of humor seems like savvy writing.

You may decide it's smarter to give this endearing quality to the best friend or sidekick rather than the protagonist. That way you can have the best of both worlds—giggles where appropriate, while not undermining the trauma or grim-jawed determination of your main character. This depends upon the tone of your book. But often even the most serious novels can benefit from a spot of humor. Readers can only endure so much misery. A wry smile now and then can alleviate the pain. A moment of humor can be a release. This is why Hitchcock heroes (or James Bond actors) often follow a tense action sense with a wry one-liner. This is why people giggle as they get off roller coasters. We've been scared. Now we're ready to laugh.

Dave Barry has used humor to great success with his articles and columns. Carl Hiaasen has used it to propel his mystery novels to great success. Needless to say, the humor, the sarcasm, the incisive commentary on Floridian lifestyles, is more important than the plotting or the unraveling of clues. The same is true of Janet Evanovich, who has climbed to stratospheric success with novels whose primary trademark is humor. People love Stephanie Plum because she makes them laugh. She has other admirable qualities, but sense of humor is the one that stands out. Anytime I've asked somebody why they enjoy Evanovich's books, the response has always ben the same. "They're funny." Young adult novels frequently have a character (often not the lead character) with a sharp sarcastic tongue—another character for the reader to identify with in a different way.

Do you have a smart aleck in your book? Can you give your protagonist a gift of wry observation? Can you use humor to attract readers to your character?

One caveat: Some people just can't do funny. If you're not funny by nature, can't tell a joke, or no one laughs when you do, then try something else. Some people who are terribly funny can't write it. One of my best writer buddies once told me that he admired the humor in my Ben Kincaid series, explaining, "I'm funny in real life. But I can't get it on the page right."

If that's you, try something else. Humorless is much better than attempts at humor that leave the reader groaning. I'm giving you five different short-term character fixes here, so you don't need them all. Focus on the ones that work for you.

The Saint

Show your character committing an act of kindness. Something for which he will receive no reward, gratitude, or recompense. Perhaps no one will even know about it (except the reader). If you really want to hammer this one home, show the character being kind to the elderly, or small children, or small animals. When we see a character treating others well, how can we not like them?

It's probably misleading for me to call this section "The Saint," because in truth, if someone becomes too saintly, they're likely to start repelling readers. A little kindness is okay. Too much aggressive kindness can be off-putting. I've read critics complaining that overtly Christian characters are often depicted in an unflattering light, but I don't think that's true. It's not Christians that are shown in a bad light, it's sanctimonious, superior, or critical people, and you can find examples of that in every religion that ever was or ever will be. So show your character committing an act of kindness, possibly without comment, and then let him get on about his business.

It's no mystery why kindness toward the elderly or the very young seems particularly poignant. These are the people in our society we think of as being most vulnerable. Personally, I've known some older folks who could kick my butt any day of the week, but that's not what we typically conjure in our minds when we hear the word "elderly." Similarly, some small children are keenly unsympathetic, like the one who's screaming two rows behind me as I'm typing this, but most of us will envision a sweet little girl in our mind's eye before we see the screeching brat.

Personally, I'm glad we live in a society that values kindness. Many good-hearted people believe the greatest accomplishments are those done in the service of others. But don't be surprised the next time you pick up a book and the hero stops on his way to the police chief's office to help a rookie file his paperwork, or the rom-com love interest stops to pick up a woman's dropped purse. In the first Christopher Reeve film, Superman is shown literally helping a cat out of a tree—for a little girl—because it would be too easy to imagine such a powerful being as completely self-absorbed or only attentive to large-scale catastrophes. An act of kindness for two small vulnerable creatures humanizes him. The plot may proceed with such alacrity that if you even thought about it, you might wonder, "What was the point of that? It didn't advance the plot." But in a way, it did. Because it subconsciously caused you to like the character a little more. And if the reader doesn't like the character, the plot can't compensate.

The Underdog

Readers root for the underdog. So make it clear from the get-go that your protagonist is an underdog, and don't let them lose that status until the story is all but over. One way to do this is to cast them into an environment or milieu in which they are oppressed or poorly treated. Another way to accomplish it is to show that the character has experienced misfortune. Undeserved misfortune.

The most obvious, and perhaps most effective, way to accomplish this is to give your protagonist a handicap, something he or she will have to overcome to accomplish their goal or desire. Who doesn't empathize with the handicapped? Handicaps can take many forms. Your character could be physically handicapped, like House or FDR. They could be mentally handicapped, like the heroes of *Flowers for Algernon* and *The Curious Incident of the Dog in the Night-Time*. Educational handicaps can be equally difficult to overcome. *Jude the Obscure* revolves around a young man desperate to attend university. Financial handicaps can be a tremendous struggle. Characters born into poverty, as in *Push* or *A Tree Grows in Brooklyn*, immediately engender our sympathy.

Again, the caution must be to avoid making the character's situation so bad that it is painful to read about, or the story becomes too maudlin. Many Dickens characters, keenly effective in their day, now seem too obviously calculated to pluck our heartstrings. You can find a compromise position. When you show your character not letting their handicap stop them from striving for their goal or desire, the handicap become part of why the reader admires the character, rather than anything maudlin or unpleasant. Some vulnerability humanizes a character. Too much makes them whiny or uncomfortable. Too little makes them unbearable.

Let's reconsider the Man of Steel. If you spend any time talking to comic book writers, virtually all will agree that the most difficult comic character to write for is Clark Kent, a.k.a., Superman. Why? Shouldn't all those powers unlock limitless plot possibilities? Yes, but they also create a problem. No vulnerability, much less a handicap. Kryptonite was introduced in the 1940s (initially on the radio show because the actor playing Superman wanted to take a vacation) to give Superman a vulnerability, but it seems too remote and convenient—i.e., since Superman is basically unstoppable, let's create a magic rock that will stop him for no logical reason. The savviest of the more recent writers have searched for vulnerability within the character himself. Books like *Superman For All Seasons* have suggested that, far from being an act, the timid, awkward, clumsy Clark Kent is who this man really is, having been raised on a Kansas farm, after all. When he goes to Metropolis (basically New York City) he's a fish out of water derided by street-smart city girl Lois Lane and others. Thus we have a brilliant irony: the most powerful man on earth has the world's biggest inferiority complex. Now that's good writing.

Can you create an underdog? Can you put your character in a situation where she has to struggle against unmerited opposition? Can you show her as the victim of undeserved misfortune? The handicaps can range from large to small. But if you can create an underdog, you may find your readers cheering for her.

CREATING CHARACTER

The Loved One

There are many virtues, but the greatest of these is love. Those acts of kindness we've discussed are evidence of a loving heart. Let's face it, we all want to be loved. It's one of the big three, that is, the universal goals or desires that all people share. We all want: 1) security (a complete illusion, at least on this side of the grave), 2) to look good (something that will never be universal), and 3) to be loved (the most obtainable, so long as you don't want it from everyone).

So it should come as no surprise that we admire those who are loved. After all, if we see someone expressing their affection to a character, we subconsciously assume they must have done something to deserve it. That makes the characters (both of them) likeable. And if you want to punch this card even harder, show your character returning the compliment. In fact, this may be vital. If your protagonist's wife of thirty-two years hugs him and says, "I love you," we immediately like both of them. But if he doesn't return the compliment, we start wondering why he's such a pig to his wife.

In what I promise will be my last reference to Sherlock Holmes (in this book), let me point out that although not everyone in the stories likes Holmes, they almost all admire him. Even poor pitiable picked-upon Lestrade admires Holmes and consults him regularly, acknowledging his enormous gifts. Watson constantly shows his love for his sometimes-roommate and boon companion, referring to him as the great detective, and the most amazing man I have ever encountered, and the greatest mind in all of England. And just to make this even better, on occasion, Holmes returns the compliment. I mean, we know he must like Watson—why else would he keep dragging the man along? Most times Watson's completely useless. But Holmes expresses his friendship repeatedly, even referring to Watson as "the finest example of the English gentleman."

In my Ben Kincaid novels, I realized from the start that some people might find Ben's timid, neurotic behavior less than heroic. This is where Christina becomes important. Because she likes him. She always liked him, from the first moment she met him. Even when he didn't much like himself, she liked him. And said so. When you've got a wonderful woman like that as your cheerleader, how can readers not admire you? If she can find his worth, so can they.

What I did not initially anticipate was that some people might not particularly like Christina. Some people, particularly female readers, found her strident or pushy. Remedy? You guessed it already. Ben likes her, too. And eventually got around to saying so. Which gives readers another reason to like her, and him as well.

Don't go overboard with these mutual admiration societies. We don't want to turn our characters into Care Bears. But if you can show that someone has earned the love and respect of another character, particularly one with perspicacity and value, that can only make him more appealing to the readers.

The Empath

Even someone outside of a relationship can be loving—and we admire those who are. Perhaps the people we admire more than any other are those who devote themselves to others, and those with a tremendous gift for forgiveness.

Think how many Biblical parables revolve around these two qualities. The story of the Good Samaritan is about devotion to others, a quality the story makes clear is often found in unexpected places (which can make for an interesting story development). The tale of the prodigal son is about forgiveness and love, regardless of the circumstances, which of course is another form of devotion to others, as opposed to indulging in petty grudges and grievances.

Showing that your character cares about others is something than can be done in few words or a brief scene. You can show the character forgiving or overlooking some personal slight just as quickly. You don't have to hammer the reader over the head with it. What you want to do is reveal the character's inner kindness, their innate instinct for self-sacrifice—something that may become more important later in the book, and perhaps even in the climax.

Don't use all of these—pick one. Possibly two. And don't mistake these quick fixes for full-fledged character. These are primarily ways to cause the reader to admire your character until you provide more profound reasons. The book is a journey, and just as your character should encounter increasingly difficult challenges along the way, their responses to those challenges should give us additional reasons to like them—and to want to read more about them.

Highlights

1) Readers must like your protagonist, either because of who they are or despite who they are, or both.

2) Readers tend to admire characters who exhibit the following traits: excellence in their work, sense of humor, kindness, triumph over adversity, affection toward and with others, and forgiveness.

Red Sneaker Exercises

1) Is your protagonist likeable? Make a list of reasons why readers should want to spend time with your character.

2) Have you planted any incidents early in the book that show your protagonist exhibiting any of the short-term fixes? If not, could you add such a scene?

3) Now consider the long term. What are the two most admirable qualities exemplified by your character? How will you make them evident over the course of the book?

4) Think of someone in real life that you admire—preferably someone you actually know. Why do you admire them? Can you inject some of those qualities into your protagonist?

5) Is there a moment when your protagonist can forgive another character—preferably one who does not really deserve it? Is there a moment when your character

can sacrifice themselves or something dear to them? Can you surprise the reader by adding an act of kindness where it is least expected?

CHAPTER 9: CHARACTER ARC

In writing…remember that the biggest stories are not written about wars, or about politics, or even murders. The biggest stories are written about the things that draw human beings closer together.

Susan Glaspell

When you plan or outline your book, always bear in mind that you are not simply charting the course of the action, or what we traditionally call the plot. You are also charting the character's journey, that is, the protagonist's development or transformation. When you outline (see discussion in Structure), your first tendency might be to focus on events, to keep the story moving. That makes sense—as a starting place. But you should also consider the impact the journey will have on your protagonist, and how they will be affected as a result. Remember that plot and character are intimately connected, so I'm not talking about two separate entities here. The character's journey is propelled by the action of the plot. The plot is motivated by the character's journey.

When I asked you to consider your protagonist's goal or desire, you probably focused on some external objective, particularly if you are planning a popular fiction novel. The amateur sleuth wants to solve the mystery of her best friend's death. The lonely romance heroine seeks true love. But now I want you to dig deeper, to penetrate further into your protagonist's skull. You filled out those job applications and completed the other character exercises for a reason—so you would know your character's life from the inside out. Now is the time to put that knowledge to use.

What does your protagonist *really* want? Sure, she wants to solve the mystery of who killed her friend...but why? Don't be content with easy answers, or empty phrases like "sense of justice" or "doing what's right." It's not enough that she has a good heart. I'm not buying that she's just curious, or a born goody-two-shoes. What compels your protagonist to take the extraordinary actions you will detail in your novel?

In other words, what is the character's journey—commonly called a character arc? Where does that arc begin? And where will it finish?

If you're planning a literary novel, or perhaps something in the realm of women's fiction, you may already be focused on the character's journey. You may already realize what your character, deep in their heart, seeks. So you may now need to focus on what events could occur during this journey. Few readers will stick long with a novel in which nothing much happens. You may be focused on emotional confrontations rather than exploding bombs, but something should be happening. Your challenge may be coming up with events that travel hand-in-hand with the inner journey to make your book satisfying.

Boarding the Arc

A character arc reveals the change a character undergoes in the course of the story.

CREATING CHARACTER

The character's journey or arc is sometimes a difficult concept for beginning writers to grasp. They have conceived of a story, primarily focused upon genre expectations, and they've got a character, so they feel ready to roll. What's this business about an arc? Why can't I just have the guy solve the mystery and be done with it? In the twenty-four books in my favorite series, those guys don't seem to be on anyone's arc. What gives?

On the other hand, some of you may have read or seen on PBS Joseph's work, starting with *The Hero With a Thousand Faces*. One of the central tenets of Campbell's work is that protagonists should be seen as metaphors (sound familiar?) and that there are recognizable patterns in their adventures. These patterns exist for a reason, and it isn't because writers are imitative. It's because stories that observe these patterns of development and growth are more satisfying, illuminating, and inspiring to readers.

Another fine writer, Christopher Vogler, has adapted Campbell's work specifically to what novelists do in a book called *The Writer's Journey*, which I highly recommend. He also identifies these common patterns and helps writers understand how they can use them to strengthen their work. One of my best writer friends, Gary Braver, has defined story as, "The young man leaves home, has adventures, slays the dragon, and comes back home again." Brilliant. The dragon, of course, is a metaphor (except in *The Hobbit*), for whatever beast your character has to overcome.

Typically, the character arc is defined in terms of the change the protagonist undergoes over the course of the book. After all, this is a journey, presumably from one thing to another, so change is essential. Typically, for these journeys to seem significant, the change should also be significant. Usually this is a dialectical journey, which Hegelian philosophers out there already know means a journey from one place to its polar opposite. Except we're not talking about physical geography here. We're talking about inner geography. We're talking about journeys of the mind and the heart.

In *To Kill a Mockingbird*, our protagonist and narrator, Scout, is a young girl in a place of relative innocence. She does not know much about the world...yet. She is about to learn. She experiences many vignettes over the course of this book—not surprising, since the novel was initially a collection of short stories. Each episode evidences Scout learning something. She learns that kindness to strangers will be ultimately rewarded. She learns it takes a brave man to stand against the mob for what he knows is right. And she learns that even the best man on earth (her father, Atticus) does not always prevail. Toward the end of the book, she learns that the monster next door may actually be a sweetheart—and the truly dangerous man might be the one who looks like everyone else. This could be boiled down to, "You can't judge a book by its cover," but why would we want to do that, when Harper Lee makes Scout's lessons come alive and seem so much more meaningful?

Is there a character arc? Is Scout on a hero's journey? Of course she is. She's travelling from innocence to maturity, from ignorance to knowledge. That's a dialectical journey from one place to its opposite. And this has enormous appeal to readers, because we can learn with her, or perhaps find reinforcement for what we already knew in our hearts was right.

Not all character journeys are so uplifting (though in the most popular novels, they typically are). Consider books like *The Great Gatsby* and *Lord of the Flies*. First, let's remember that the protagonist of Gatsby is not the title character but Nick Carraway, who is living not far from the Gatsby compound. Nick is dazzled by the gorgeous, successful, and fabulously rich Gatsby. To him, Gatsby embodies the American Dream, the rags-to-riches story of a young man making a success of himself through his own hard work and pluck. This dazzling figure has it all, or so it seems. The more time he spends with Gatsby, however, the more Nick realizes that Gatsby does not have it all—in fact, he does not have the one thing he wants most, the love of his life, Daisy. And at the end, Gatsby is killed in a sorry case of mistaken identity. Turns out, the American Dream wasn't all it was cracked up to be.

Lord of the Flies is even more disheartening. Take a bunch of nice boys from a good school and crash them on a deserted island, free from the strictures of society, and what happens? They become savages. Without the civilizing influences of law and society, they revert to a primitive, tribal state. They compete brutally with one another. They worship a ludicrous pagan god. The bitterness and rivalry eventually leads to murder. These boys learn something about themselves (as we do), but there's nothing nice about the lesson.

In both *Gatsby* and *Flies*, the main characters are on a dialectical journey, but unlike the journey in *Mockingbird*, they are travelling from a relatively good place to a negative one. Nick becomes disillusioned with all he previously held to be true and desirable. The boys in *Flies* learn how tenuous the British gentleman really is, how quickly he reverts to animalistic behavior once removed from governing influences. These journeys are backwards around the world from the journey of Scout. These are stories in which the emperor learns that he has no clothes. These are journeys from having something to believe in to utter disillusionment.

I can't end this section on such a depressing note. Let's consider another possible journey. Have you read *Lord Jim* by Joseph Conrad? Let me ask it another way. Have you started *Lord Jim*? This is probably the world's most frequently started but not finished book (excepting all those who quit James Joyce's *Ulysses* in chapter three). The many levels of diegesis and chronological hopscotch make it a challenging read. But don't give up. Tough it out. It's worth it.

Lord Jim is an officer on a British sailing vessel at a time when England rules the seas. His ship is caught in a bad storm. The captain and officers decide to abandon ship. They climb into a lifeboat, leaving the rest of the crew behind. This is bad enough—the captain and officers are supposed to go down with the ship. But to make matters worse, the ship does not sink. The crew manages to get it to shore. Talk about red faces. Lord Jim and the others are court-martialed. End of the story? No.

Many years later, we hear of a mysterious white man who is helping natives in Southeast Asia in their struggle against a vicious warlord. He eventually gives his life to save them. They have no idea why. But we do. We realize this is the court-martialed Jim, trying to prove he is not a coward. Jim knows he has committed an unpardonable error and now he's trying to redeem himself.

This journey is different from the one Scout undertook, but it's still a movement in a positive direction. This is a journey from disquiet to contentment, from sin to redemption. Like the education journey, this gives readers enormous satisfaction for two reasons. First, it gives

110

readers an adrenaline surge to vicariously experience someone else's redemption. Second—it provides a balm to all those who have made titanic mistakes, which would be just about everyone. And we would all like to believe there's some way to compensate, some way to atone. Thus the appeal of the redemption arc.

This is far from a complete list of all the journeys your character can travel. All that matters is that your character does make a journey, that it seems like a significant one, and that even though you don't explicitly spell it out, the reader comprehends that the protagonist has changed, has been influenced, by the events of the book. It makes a story seem more significant, more than just a handful of engaging events. It's what distinguishes an incident, or episode, from a *story*.

Series Books

I have often been asked how this applies to writers penning a series. By series, I mean many self-contained books sharing the same protagonist, not one story that is continued over many books. Too often people have been advised, sometimes by speakers in a position to know better, that they should never let their protagonist change. Why? Because they want readers to be able to pick up the books and read them in any order without difficulty.

I think this is fantastically bad advice.

Sure, it can be done, and there are some examples of it out there (which I won't name). But these people are not in tune with the contemporary audience. These people still perceive books with a series character as a sort of literary chewing gum, something to pass the time and then be spit out quickly when the flavor has faded. These people are still thinking of their books like episodes in older television series. Indeed, in those series, protagonists rarely changed, because the producers knew they couldn't expect viewers to catch every episode, and there were few chances to revisit an episode you'd missed, so every episode ended with a reboot taking the characters back to square one. The case is closed for good. If the hero falls in love, she dies by the final fadeout. So the next episode can start in the same place as every other one.

I don't even think this was a good approach for a television series, but I think it's a disastrous approach for books. Have you noticed that more and more of the modern TV programs—particularly the enormously popular cable shows—are moving toward long-term continuing stories, rather than every-episode reboots? I have. I think there's an increasingly sophisticated audience tired of the same old repetitious episodic junk, hungering for stories with greater depth. And I think we're starting to see that happening with books as well. From the get-go, books have struggled to compete with television, which delivers its stories in a far less demanding, entirely passive manner. That will only become worse if series books cling to an archaic storytelling model.

The idea of character arc is not inherently incompatible with the idea of a series character. It just means that, for each volume in the series, the character must go on a different journey. Fortunately, we are all complex people, and our lives encompass many journeys, many learning experiences, many quests for completion or redemption. So there's no reason why a character should ever run out of them. In the Ben Kincaid series, I have tried to bear in mind that regardless of the plot or the client, the protagonist is Ben. Therefore, the story must at its core be about Ben. It must affect him personally, not just professionally. He can't be a guest star in his own book. Therefore, for each volume, I found a new journey.

Not all journeys are necessarily resolved in a single volume (although there should be something in each volume to give it a feeling of reader satisfaction). In the first book, *Primary Justice*, I intimated that Ben had endured strong conflicts with his recently deceased father, who disinherited him. Very little is actually revealed about the problem in that book. It's not the main plot. But I trickled hints along the way, hoping the reader would keep track. In the sixth book in the series, *Naked Justice*, I decided it was time to let this conflict come to the forefront. The reader learns all the gruesome details about Ben's abusive father...and in the course of the adventure, Ben comes to a better place, one of acceptance and forgiveness. And having made that journey, the business with his father is never mentioned again, not in any of the subsequent volumes.

I don't know if it helped sales or hurt them, but I never let the Kincaid series do a complete "reboot." I was determined at all times to have the main character move forward. I couldn't stand the thought of these people who were so real to me perpetually running in place like hamsters on a wheel. So after the first book, Ben leaves the big law firm. At the end of the second, he establishes his own firm. At the end of the sixth, he gives up his practice (it doesn't last). At the end of the twelfth, he and Christina begin dating. And at the start of the sixteenth, they marry. Get the idea? No hamsters. There's still no reason why a reader couldn't read the books out of order. But Ben went on appropriate character journeys (and some of the other characters, like Christina, Loving, and Mike did, too). Each book is a real novel, not just the next episode.

At a speaking engagement for *Capitol Offense*, a crusty old guy in the back row asked me, "Why'd you go and have Ben get married?" I could see he was displeased about this event, though I wasn't sure if it was because he wanted the character to always remain the same or because he had personally found marriage so gruesome. I'll bet you can guess my response.

"What did you think was going to happen? They'd been flirting for fifteen novels."

The Joy of Creation

Character creation can be one of the most challenging aspects of writing, but also one of the most fun. Bringing fictional entities to life may be the ultimate act of creation for humans. Sure, you can have children, but do you get to sculpt their personalities from the ground up? Probably not. With fictional characters, you can embody a metaphor that has meaning to you, pick and choose from a wide variety of traits, assign characteristics that make it all seem real, and set them on meaningful journeys with closure and change—something that all too often eludes us in real life.

If you haven't started writing yet, or even if you have, commit to a daily writing schedule. Sign the contract you'll find in Appendix C. Have it witnessed by someone who will support you. Look at the week-by-week writing guidelines found in Appendix B and get started. I don't know how long it will take you to finish this book. But I know you will never finish until you start.

Any time you ask someone why they loved a book, more likely than not, the answer will involve the lead character. Make your next character just as memorable as the ones you've loved in the past. Bring your story to life

Highlights

1) A character arc reveals the change a character undergoes in the course of the story.

2) Most character arcs involve a dialectical journey from one place to its opposite, i.e., from innocence to maturity, or from ignorance to wisdom.

3) Even series characters should have character arcs.

Red Sneaker Exercises

1) How does your character change over the course of the story? What character arc does this represent? Is your character travelling from one place to its opposite?

2) Many beginning writers unconsciously pen coming-of-age stories. In other words, the character arc is the journey from ignorance (of something) to knowledge. Does your protagonist grow over the course of the book? Does he learn something he did not realize before?

3) In the book on Structure, I suggested planning a Character Turning Point somewhere in the middle of the second act. This is the point when the reader may start to detect the character's shift from one position to its opposite—though it is far from fully realized, and may not be fully realized till the last page of the book. Does your book have a Character Turning Point? If not, can you add one?

APPENDIX A: Character Detail Sheet

Name (Nickname?)

Address

Physical Appearance (hair color, eye color, etc.)

Manner of Speaking

Place of Birth

Other Places You Have Lived (and why)

Ethnic Background

Family Background

Notable Moments from Childhood

Educational Background

Relationship with Family

Married/Divorced/Single

Children?

Pets?

Favorite Foods

Hobbies

Special Interests

Favorite Music

Favorite Television Show

Favorite Movie

Favorite Book

Special Skills or Abilities

Vices

Employment History

Philosophy of Life

Who are you closest to?

If you could have one of Superman's powers, which one would it be?

What makes you angry? What makes you laugh?

What do you do when you're angry?

CREATING CHARACTER

Have you ever been in love? How often? What happened?

What do you fear most? Who else knows about this fear?

What's in your refrigerator?

What books are on your nightstand?

What is your favorite food?

What's your favorite smell?

What does your clothes closet look like?

What car do you drive? What does it look like inside?

What did you have for breakfast?

What do you do on Friday nights?

What do you remember best about your childhood?

What do you consider your greatest achievement?

What is your idea of perfect happiness?

What is your most cherished possession?

When and where were you happiest?

What do you most despise?

Who do you most dislike?

What is your greatest regret?

Which talent or ability would you most like to have?

What is the trait you most despise in yourself?

What is the trait you most despise in others?

Who is your favorite fictional hero?

Whose are your real-life heroes?

Have you even told a lie? When and why?

Which words or phrases do you tend to overuse?

If you could change one thing about yourself, what would it be?

If you were to die and come back, who or what would you like to be the second time around?

APPENDIX B: The Writer's Calendar

Is it possible to finish a top-quality manuscript in six months? Of course it is, if you're willing to do the work necessary to make it happen. Here's how you do it.

Week 1
Commit to your writing schedule.
Find your studio.
Sign the Writer's Contract in Appendix C. Inform friends and family.
Think about what you want to write. Start thinking like a writer.

Week 2
Commit to a premise—then make it bigger. Is it big and unique enough to attract a publisher?
Commit to a genre. What's your spin on the genre? How will you make it the same—but different? Research as needed.

Week 3
Develop your main protagonist and antagonist.
Complete Character Detail Sheets (in Appendix A) for both. What are their best qualities—and worst? What drives them?
What is your protagonist's character arc? What does he/she want, seek, desire?

Write a half-page example of dialogue for each major character in their distinct voice.

Week 4
Put all major events (Scenes) on index cards, approximately sixty total (as described in the Red Sneaker book on Structure).

Arrange cards by Acts. Highlight the Plot Turning Points and Character Turning Points.

Type the index cards into an outline, adding detail when you have it.

Week 5
Think about the shape of your story—the Plot. Will your character experience growth? Maturity? Redemption? Disillusionment? (Reference Red Sneaker book on Plot)

Map out twists and turns to maintain reader interest. What is the last occurrence the reader will suspect?

Don't shy away from a great scene because it doesn't fit your story as you currently understand it. See if you can change the story to accommodate the great scene.

Weeks 6-18
Write at least five pages every day—ten on Saturdays. No editing. Just keep moving ahead.

Do additional writing as necessary to complete 10% each week.

Week 19-21
Perform triage on what you've written. Revise. Then revise more. Reference the Revision lecture on the *Fundamentals of Fiction* DVD to spot potential problems.

CREATING CHARACTER

Week 22-24

Give the manuscript to trusted reader(s).

Reread it yourself, focusing on character consistency, character depth. Are the characters sympathetic or empathetic?

Reread it focusing on plot, pacing, story logic, theme. Is the story plausible? Obtain comments from readers. Incorporate comments from readers where appropriate.

Reread it focusing on dialogue.

Set it aside, then reread it with fresh eyes. Do you see problems you didn't spot before?

And then—

Attend writing conferences and bounce your ideas off agents and editors. If people don't ask to see your manuscript, your premise needs work. If people ask to see pages but don't take you on, it suggests your manuscript is not yet ready. Consider attending a small-group writing seminar to give your book that final push it needs to be publishable.

APPENDIX C: The Writer's Contract

I, _____, hereinafter known as "the Writer," in consideration of these premises, hereby agree as follows:

1) The aforementioned Writer hereby agrees that he/she will undertake a long-term, intensive writing project. The Writer agrees to work ____ hours a day, regardless of external distractions or personal circumstances. The Writer agrees to maintain this schedule until the writing project is completed.

2) The Writer understands that this is a difficult task and that there will be days when he/she does not feel like writing or when others will make demands upon the Writer's time. The Writer will not allow this to interfere with the completion of the agreement made in paragraph one (1) of this contract.

3) The Writer also understands that good physical and mental health is essential to the completion of any writing project. Therefore, in order to complete the agreement made in paragraph one (1), the Writer commits to a serious program of self-care, which shall include but shall not be limited to: adequate sleep, healthy diet, exercise, the relinquishment of bad habits, and reading time.

Signature of the Writer and Witnesses/Date

APPENDIX D: The Writer's Reading List

The Chicago Manual on Style. 15th ed. Chicago: University of Chicago Press, 2003.

Cook, Vivian. *All in a Word: 100 Delightful Excursions into the Uses and Abuses of Words*. Brooklyn: Melville House, 2010.

Fowler, H.W. *A Dictionary of Modern English Usage*. 2nd ed. Rev. Ernest Gowers. N.Y. & Oxford: Oxford University Press, 1965.

Hale, Constance. *Sin and Syntax: How to Create Wickedly Effective Prose*. New York: Broadway Books, 2001.

Hart, Jack. *A Writer's Coach: The Complete Guide to Writing Strategies That Work*. New York: Anchor Books, 2006.

Jones, Catherine Ann. *The Way of Story: The Craft and Soul of Writing*. Studio City: Michael Wiese Productions, 2007.

Klauser, Henriette Anne. *Writing on Both Sides of the Brain*. San Francisco: Harper & Row, 1987.

Maass, Donald. *The Fire in Fiction: Passion, Purpose, and Techniques to Make Your Novel Great.* Cincinnati: Writers Digest Books, 2009.

Maass, Donald. *Writing the Breakout Novel: Insider Advice for Taking Your Fiction to the Next Level.* Cincinnati, Writers Digest Books, 2001.

Maass, Donald. *Writing 21st Century Fiction: High Impact Techniques for Exceptional Storytelling.* Cincinnati: Writers Digest Books, 2012.

O'Conner, Patricia T. *Woe Is I: The Grammarphobe's Guide to Better English in Plain English.* 2nd ed. New York: Riverhead Books, 2003.

O'Conner, Patricia T. *Origins of the Specious: Myths and Misconceptions of the English Language.* New York: Random House, 2009.

Strunk, William, Jr., and White, E.B. *The Elements of Style.* 4th ed. N.Y.: Macmillan, 2000.

About the Author

William Bernhardt is the bestselling author of more than thirty novels, including the blockbuster Ben Kincaid series of legal thrillers. In addition, Bernhardt founded the Red Sneaker Writing Center in 2005, hosting writing workshops and small-group seminars and becoming one of the most in-demand writing instructors in the nation. His programs have educated many authors now published at major New York houses. He holds a Masters Degree in English Literature and is the only writer to have received the Southern Writers Guild's Gold Medal Award, the Royden B. Davis Distinguished Author Award (University of Pennsylvania) and the H. Louise Cobb Distinguished Author Award (Oklahoma State), which is given "in recognition of an outstanding body of work that has profoundly influenced the way in which we understand ourselves and American society at large." In addition to the novels, he has written plays, including a musical (book and music), humor, nonfiction books, children books, and crossword puzzles. He also has published many poems and is a member of the American Academy of Poets.

24619950R00091

Made in the USA
Middletown, DE
30 September 2015